Penguin Handbooks
The Pauper's Cookbook

KU-317-554

Jocasta Innes was born in Nanking, China, and by the age of twelve had visited every continent in the world. She was chiefly educated at Bedford High School and at Girton College, Cambridge. For some years she worked as a feature writer on the *Evening Standard*. Now married to novelist Joe Potts, she lives in Swanage, Dorset, and has four children, two by a previous marriage. She has always taken a greedy interest in food, and learned to cook in a hit-or-miss fashion from books, starting with the tricky stuff and working backwards to the point where sensible people begin. She reckons that she graduated to serious or creative cooking in the last five years, and finds being hard-up a genuine stimulus and challenge where cooking is concerned: more work, perhaps, but infinitely greater satisfaction. Her previous literary work mainly consists of translations from French and Spanish and she has recently written a book on Eastern cooking on a budget, to be published in Penguins. *The Pauper's Homemaking Book* was published in Penguins in 1976. Her other interests are gardening, swimming and collecting junk.

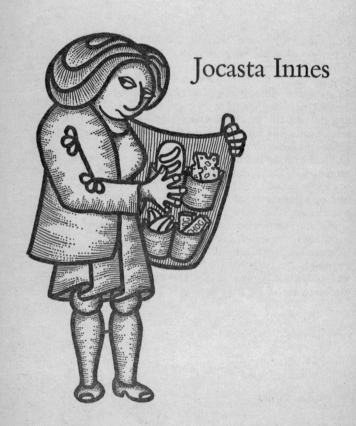

Jocasta Innes

The
Pauper's
Cookbook

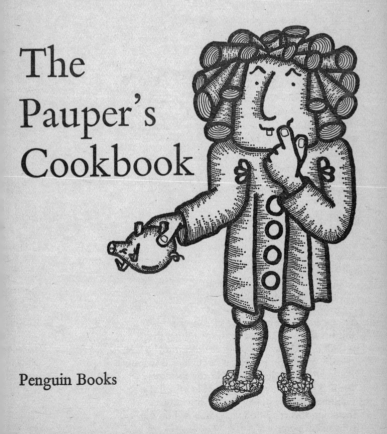

Penguin Books

Penguin Books Ltd, Harmondsworth,
Middlesex, England
Penguin Books, 625 Madison Avenue,
New York, New York 10022, U.S.A.
Penguin Books Australia Ltd, Ringwood,
Victoria, Australia
Penguin Books Canada Ltd, 2801 John Street,
Markham, Ontario, Canada L3R 1B4
Penguin Books (N.Z.) Ltd, 182–190 Wairau Road,
Auckland 10, New Zealand

First published 1971
Reprinted 1971, 1973, 1974, 1975, 1976 (twice), 1977, 1978
Reprinted with revisions 1979

Copyright © Jocasta Innes, 1971
All rights reserved

Set, printed and bound in Great Britain by
Cox & Wyman Ltd.,
London, Reading and Fakenham
Set in Monotype Bembo

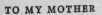

TO MY MOTHER

Contents

Acknowledgements

My first attempt at 'real' cooking was, I remember, an Estouffade de Bœuf à la Provençale from Elizabeth David's *French Country Cooking*. It was a happy accident which put me in the way of Mrs David's excellent book but no accident at all, as countless other devotees will corroborate, that the dish turned out a success. I would like to take this opportunity of thanking Mrs David for that auspicious start, for the inspiration and pleasure her books have given me since – which is reflected in several of the recipes in this book – but above all for demonstrating so convincingly that intelligence, taste and imagination have as much to do with cookery as with any other art.

Next I would like to thank that adventurous and gifted cook, my mother, for her generous help and good-humoured advice and encouragement in the writing of this book and of course for having insidiously implanted in me over the years a healthy appetite for good food. Also my father, who did his best to relieve me of a stubborn mental block, towards the intricacies of comparative weights and measures.

My thanks are also due to Bronwen Cunningham, May Crittall, Peter Stickland, Claudia Maxtone Grahame, Paul Winstanley, Kathleen Marsh, Jack Hollingshead, Christine Goodwin, all of whom contributed ideas, advice or criticism. To my sister, Judy Astor, who set the ball rolling. To Mike Spink for the drawings. And special thanks to my bank manager, Mr White, without whose patient cooperation this book might never have been written. And lastly to Joe, who had to eat his way through the book.

Introduction

I suppose I have been waiting for someone to write a cookbook like this one ever since I started to cook. The trouble with the lovely readable cookbooks I had was that they were written for people with some cooking experience and enough money to experiment, which put them right out of my class. I was much too green to see this. I was also greedy, and rather stubborn. I'm quite astonished to think how often I must have bounced confidently into the kitchen, mind aglow with imagined treats in store, to set about massacring yet another culinary masterpiece. I did learn to cook in the end, but backwards, starting at the haute cuisine end and slowly retreating to the point where I should have begun, acquiring basic skills like pastry making and learning to plan and cook well-balanced meals on a small budget.

What I could have done with, right from the start, was a cookbook with quite a different approach, tailored to the tastes *and* limitations of a greedy pauper. No talk of truffles and peach-fed hams and chickens simmered in champagne in this book to lead them astray or make them discontented. But no half-hearted trickery with a tin opener and a pinch of herbs either. This book would deal with good solid rewarding food *but* – and this would be its great advantage to people like myself – all the recipes would be so cheap that one would be imperceptibly, painlessly conditioned to buy and cook economically and well. It stood to reason that there must be a good few other people in my situation, trying to conjure good food from limited cash, battered old pots and pans and kitchens more nightmarish than dream. What a blessing for us all such a book would be, I thought, and waited for some highly qualified expert to leap in and write it.

Well, time passed and no one took up the challenge, and my cooking improved, though I say it myself, beyond all recognition. Then it suddenly occurred to me that the shortest answer to the whole problem would be to write a pauper's cookbook myself. Why not? I might not have any diplomas, but diplomas seemed less relevant to the problems of cooking on the cheap than first-hand experience, and I had plenty of that. Congenital greed had stimulated me into a great deal of experiment with bargain meals, which had taught me a lot, while the candid comments of those around had kept my standards up. From talking about it I somehow fell into planning and writing it, and so here at last is a cookbook written specially for greedy paupers, with my good wishes and hopes that it will ease others into a more comfortable frame of mind, purse and stomach.

Money. The cheapest meals in the book cost less than 20p a head. By meal I mean a solid main dish, with appropriate trimmings. These bargains are marked throughout the book with an asterisk for speedy reference in hard times. The most expensive recipes, assembled under the heading Fancy Work, might cost twice that. The rest come somewhere between. Thus a typical three-course meal based on recipes in this book should set you back a bit less than eating in a transport cafe, and you can't, in these inflationary days, say much fairer than that. Should you need to slash costs still further, you can concentrate on meatless or asterisked dishes, use marge instead of butter, vegetable instead of olive oil, and cut fuel bills by planning meals which can be cooked simultaneously on different grids in the oven. The chapter Programmed Eating may help you there.

The recipes I have chosen are a mixed bunch in every sense, international – European, Chinese, American – and democratic, ranging all the way up the social scale from hearty peasant fare to delicate country-house collations. Aside from cheapness and niceness, qualification for entry depended on scoring high marks on a time-and-effort v. results test. In other words, more time and trouble had to produce proportionately splendid results, or the recipe was out. (This cannot be said of all marathon recipes which worm their way into even the best cookbooks.) I do understand that people can't be forever chopping and stirring and peering into ovens. It must be said, however, that those who expect proper food to materialize in the time it takes to warm a tin of baked beans are optimists, or philistines. When time presses, consult Fast Work, a chapter of recipes which can be prepared and cooked at the double. People who would rather get the cooking over in one furious burst, and knock off the rest of the week should study the seven-day menus in the chapter on Programmed Eating, designed primarily for working wives. For those occasions when you want to Create, not just cook, I have included some challenging items in the Fancy Work section, all of which – Chinese Pancakes in particular – passed the above-mentioned test with honours.

Finally, a few words about the plan of this book, which may seem a bit bewildering if you are used to the usual system of grouping items generically, i.e., soups, fish, eggs, meat, etc. This system is practical for the experienced cook, who has no difficulty choosing between thirty different ways of cooking eggs, or chicken, or apples; but even then, I think, it makes large demands on one's time. When you simply want ideas for a big dish for lots of people, or a light snack for two, it is maddening to have to sort through pages of alternatives. A more practical approach, I decided, would be to work out certain basic cooking situations and group together the recipes best suited to dealing with them. The plan I evolved goes like this –

1. *Standards:* Large selection of recipes covering all the components of a three-course meal, including vegetables, salads and a few sauces, all chosen because they are the sort of food you can eat over and over again without boredom. Ideal dishes to learn on.

2. *Padding:* This deals with what you add to the leftovers you have, to make them into a square meal. Paupers should read this section because padding techniques are central to thrifty cookery.

3. *Fast Work:* Collection of quickly made dishes, based on tinned food or materials usually to hand.

4. *Programmed Eating:* General advice on how to plan meals seven days ahead, doing most of the cooking in one operation, with four suggested weekly plans as an illustration.

5. *Private Enterprise:* Pleasant money-saving extras to make when you are in the mood – jams, biscuits, etc. – plus some ideas for living off the land, mainly for country dwellers.

6. *Fancy Work:* Recipes for special occasions, some fancier, some exotic, some more expensive. Also advice on planning a well-balanced meal.

7. *Dieting on the Cheap:* A collection of cheap, low-calorie ideas for slimmers.

I have also included a short chapter on equipment, from the angle of how little you can get away with, rather than how much you need, and some suggestions for shopping intelligently and economically, in the chapter Where the Money Goes. Shopping, if you set about it the right way, is where the saving starts, as well as where the money goes.

Where the Money Goes

Indisputably, it goes. But it is possible to control the outflow and see that you get value for your money. Sensible shopping, the domestic equivalent of a planned economy, does save actual money, largely by cutting down on wastage, and it should also ensure that you have good quality materials to cook with.

Without going to the lengths of keeping itemized accounts of everything you spend, you will need to introduce a little system into your spending to avoid fetching up broke and hungry halfway through the week. The first thing is to decide how much you want, or can afford, to spend on food each week. Make a rough estimate of your weekly consumption of essentials like bread, butter, eggs, tea, milk, and what this costs. Subtract the figure from your weekly budget, divide the remainder by seven, and you are left with a pretty good idea of what your daily expenditure should be. If you keep well within this figure half the week, you will have accumulated enough to buy something special for the week-end, or stock up on tins, extra herbs, sauces, etc.

A shopping list is the most effective curb on over-stepping your daily food budget. Decide what you are going to eat, check the recipe against what you have already got, list what you need, and *stick* to the list. Elementary, I know, but for every steel-trap mind there must be ten impulse buyers bumbling round the shops, trusting to association of ideas to come up with the right answer. A fallible system at any time, and positively dangerous in supermarkets. On the other hand, don't become too inflexible – if a good buy crops up unexpectedly, stewing veal, say, or sprats, you should be able to revise your other purchases accordingly. A little homework with this cookbook ought to help there.

Shop around for shops. The delicatessen round the corner may be handy, but convenience shops like these tend to bump up their prices. Supermarkets are immensely convenient, and their own lines in groceries and dairy products are often good buys, but I still think paupers are better off getting meat, fish, greenstuffs and bread at shops which specialize in these things and carry a wider range of alternatives, most of which are fresher and many of which are cheaper than the more standardized supermarket selection. Before deciding which shops to patronize, compare prices and the range and quality of goods on display. The butcher for you is one who stocks a wide range of good-quality cheap cuts as well as offal, rabbit, pigeons. Your fishmonger should offer bargains like mussels and sprats in season. Your greengrocer ought to stock a selection of local produce (this applies less to large towns of course) as well as imported stuff. Generalizations are risky, but, on the whole, I find the smaller family business tends to be more enterprising than the chain stores, pricier at the upper end of their range, but with more to offer at the lower.

Where two shops are much of a muchness, go for the one with the friendlier staff. Having made your choice, try and stick to it. Shopkeepers take more trouble over their regulars. As a regular customer, too, you are in a stronger position when it comes to complaining about inferior goods—mouldy tomatoes, say, or rubberoid meat. Don't be afraid to do so – I suspect many paupers develop an inferiority complex about the small sums they spend but this is unrealistic because for every big spender there must be crowds of modest ones, as shopkeepers well know. Besides, you may not always be a pauper, and they bear this in mind too. Don't make scenes or become abusive but show that you are concerned to get value for your money and a sensible shopkeeper will treat you with greater respect.

Paupers, my mother crisply observed, cannot afford to be squeamish, and she has a point. Don't be cowardly about trying something new, odd, or unprepossessing-looking. Most shoppers go for the obvious, safe and familiar, particularly in the meat line – chops and frying steak, according to my butcher – with the result that these get pricier while offbeat items are often absurdly cheap. The less snob cuts of meat like shin of beef, ox cheek, hand of pork, many varieties of game, and most of what goes under the unfortunate name of 'offal' – brains, liver, hearts, etc. – are all excellent buys, delicious eating when properly cooked (you will find many suggestions in the book) and good food value. In the fish line you should try mussels, sprats, coley, bream, as well as mackerel and herring. And I often find the humbler vegetables like kale and spring greens more rewarding, carefully cooked, than jaded and more expensive foreign imports.

A list of economical buys you might find useful.

Cooking Oil: I use the cheapest vegetable oil I can find, sold in 7-gallon drums, for cooking and salad dressing. To give olive oil flavour, pack a jar with black olives and fill up with oil – keep for making vinaigrette.

Bacon: Cheapest, and nicest, I find is ordinary streaky bacon cut extra thin. Grocers where they slice their own will do this for you. You get more rashers this way, and – being so thin – they fry up delectably crisp. Cook them slowly, over moderate heat, and the fat which runs off should be enough to fry eggs, tomatoes and bread. Lard, which spoils the flavours, is unnecessary.

Tea: For a fragrant tea with body to it mix Earl Grey with one of the cheapest strong Tips, in whatever proportions appeal to you – one Earl Grey to two Tips is good.

Coffee: Instant is cheapest, but only a ghost of the real thing. Try the coffee-and-chicory blends, cheapest in the ground-coffee range.

Butter: Cheap butter is cheap enough, I think, to warrant using it for all purposes, though lard and marge are useful for pastry. I find most cheap brands too salty. Many stores stock a brand called Creamery Butter, which costs very little more than the cheapest butters and contains less salt.

Rice: Get the cheapest long-grain available. It doesn't look so elegant but it is cheaper than the packet type, and quite adequate if you cook it properly. (*See* Rice, p. 86.)

Marmalade: Home-made is best, and cheapest. Next best thing is South African, packed in 2 lb. tins. Conscientious liberals may object, but it is much fruitier than the shreds in jelly type, and half the price of the snob brands.

Gammon: Idling round ham and bacon counters may produce unconsidered trifles. Bacon knuckles, for instance. Good for flavouring minestrone, or bean dishes. Odd scraps of ham and bacon left from slicing can be had for next to nothing, too.

Markets: It is always worth tracking down the time and place of local markets. Good selection of fruit and veg., usually cheap and fresh. Fish and shellfish, particularly in the London area. I am told – but don't count on this – that if you wander along just before closing-up time you can get the same goods cheaper still because the stallholders want to clear their stocks.

Health-food Stores: If your shopping facilities are unimaginative, a health-food store can often fill the gaps. They specialize in herbs, pulses, yoghourt. Their raw-sugar chocolate costs a bit more, but it is excellent for cooking.

Shopping is the most tedious aspect of good eating, but the cleverer you get at it, the more time and money you save, and the element of challenge that enters when you are executing a coolly premeditated plan of action – like guerrilla fighting, clever shopping requires quick reflexes, resourcefulness and a cool head – makes the business much more amusing.

Stocking Up

The following is an indication of what you may need in the way of tins, herbs, cereals and other ingredients, when following the recipes in the book. There is no need to rush out and buy them all at once. I have italicized the items most constantly in demand. If you can grow any herbs yourself so much the better – a windowbox of herbs gives a magical lift to pauper cookery. The dried variety last a long time though, and are so pungent you need only a pinch at a time. Tinned foods are essential if you go in for last-minute meals (Fast Work) and most paupers are advised to have a few on hand for emergencies.

Tins: Tuna, crab, salmon, anchovies, corned beef, *peeled tomatoes, tomato purée*, pilchards.

Dried Fruit: Raisins, *sultanas*, prunes, apricots.

Sauces, condiments, etc.: Dry mustard, *vinegar,* curry paste (Vindaloo paste is tremendously appetizing, sparingly used) or powder, *Worcestershire Sauce, soy sauce,* capers, Anchovy Essence.

Herbs: Thyme, *sage, bayleaves,* tarragon, marjoram, basil. Dried parsley is tasteless, better to buy it fresh and store it in a polythene bag in the fridge or larder. Damp it first and it will keep for days.

Spices: Black pepper (your own mill and pepper corns are best, but the ground variety will do), *cinnamon,* juniper berries, mace, allspice, coriander seeds, ginger, *vanilla essence,* or, better still, pods.

Pulses (dried peas and beans): Keep a selection of the following – lentils, haricot beans, split peas, chick peas, navy beans.

Cereals: Rice, *pasta* (Lily brand is a reliable make), *flour, corn-flour,* pearl barley, oatmeal.

It is better to buy cereals and pulses in smallish quantities and replace them because they deteriorate with time.

You will also need a constant supply of lemons (the pauper's answer to wine marinades), cooking oil, garlic, breadcrumbs (make your own by drying stale bread slowly in the bottom of the oven, pounding, sieving or grating it to crumb consistency. Store in an airtight tin or jar.) Cheddar – mousetrap – will serve for cheesy dishes (except gnocchi, which must have Parmesan, preferably bought in the lump and grated) but a mixture of Cheddar and a more refined cheese – Gloucester, Edam, Cheshire – is better still. For puddings, cakes, etc., buy the cheapest block cooking chocolate.

Vanilla Sugar: This improves most puddings, cakes and biscuits, used in place of ordinary granulated or caster sugar. You can make your own very easily by buying a few vanilla pods from a good grocer or delicatessen and storing them in a covered jar or tin of caster sugar. Label the tin or jar, so that you don't use the sugar for sweetening tea by mistake. The vanilla pods can be used for flavouring milk puddings and custards, rinsed and put back in the jar. They can be used three or four times.

Wherewithal

Improvisation is the key-word here. Paupers are often pushed for space as well as cash and the logical answer is to have a minimum of equipment, which can double up for different purposes.

Storage: Simplest, cheapest and handiest way of keeping it out of the way when not in use is to borrow a practical French trick and hang as much as possible from hooks, or plain nails, in the walls.

If you are short of working surfaces, and your kitchen space can accommodate another piece of furniture, look for a low cupboard (waist-height, or lower) in a junk shop. Cover it with formica, or a slab of marble off an old washstand – the latter makes the ideal pastry board. The cupboard will take casseroles, etc., and groceries.

Where to buy: Junk shops, Oxfam shops, jumble sales, are fruitful locales for kitchen equipment. For once the consumer society works in your favour. Households which have gone mad for stainless steel, and enamelled cast-iron, often throw out a mass of serviceable pots, pans and utensils. Dingy to look at, perhaps, but often surprisingly good quality. Weight is a reliable indication of quality – the heavier your saucepan or casserole, the better it holds and diffuses heat.

Look out for: aluminium and copper pans, cast-iron (rare but excellent) and stoneware casseroles, the latter usually brown or green outside, cream within. They often arrive lidless, but inverted plates or foil will substitute in most cases. You can't have too many china mixing bowls – a 'slight fault' doesn't matter if you don't bash it too heartily. Glass storage jars (must have tops) and canisters are useful for storing perishable foods. Bread boards, rolling pins, carving knives, are all worth looking out for. Antiquated gadgets, if you can work out what they are *for*, are often good buys and usually work very efficiently with a little cleaning and oiling.

For anything else, try Woolworth's or a good ironmongers.

WHAT YOU WILL NEED

The following is a skeleton selection of equipment but it should prove adequate for the recipes in this book. Again, there is no need to buy all of it at once – keep adding to it as occasion arises and cash permits.

Cooking Knife: One thing you cannot do without. It should be medium size, sharp as a razor, and good quality. You need it for slicing and trimming meat, chopping vegetables, herbs, peeling potatoes, de-rinding bacon, and a host of other jobs. Quality pays off here. If you can't wangle one as a present, save up, and in the meantime hunt up an old-fashioned non-stainless kitchen knife in a junk shop and sharpen it regularly on a carborundum. Stainless, serrated-edge knives are adequate for peeling and scraping vegetables, but not much else.

Chopping Board: Also essential. The back of a wooden bread board will do. Scrub it often or you will find garlic permeating everything.

Saucepans: Two is the minimum. One medium-to-large, one a size or two smaller. The big one for soups, pasta, rice, which need a lot of liquid. Smaller one for vegetables, etc. You can improvise a double boiler by standing the smaller inside the larger one. A very small pan is best for boiling eggs, milk, sauces.

Casseroles: Two again. Big one for stews, pot roasts and bulky dishes. Smaller (quart size) for milk puddings, pâtés, soufflés, fish pie, etc. I find stoneware the most versatile material for the money.

Sieve: A fairly capacious one for sieving, or puréeing soup, sauces, stewed fruit, flour. Metal is strongest, good quality plastic adequate, as long as you don't hold it over direct heat. You need a hair sieve for sieving acidy fruit.

Colander: People muddle along without, by juggling with saucepan lids or plates, but colanders save time and scalds and you can pick them up cheaply in junk shops – the metal ones are better than your gay plastics, as they don't melt.

Frying Pan: One medium-sized one will cope with most frying jobs. It should be a heavyweight one, but the Woolworth's kind is adequate if you use it with an asbestos mat, to prevent food sticking and burning. Non-stick are more trouble than they are worth.

Roasting Pan: The cheapest is all right. A medium-sized pan will take shepherd's pie, upside-down puddings, as well as roasts.

Grill Pan: Some elderly cookers have lost their grill pans. You need one though, for grilling meat, as well as toasting bread.

Mixing Bowls: One sturdy, large one for mixing batters, meat-loaf ingredients, etc. A small one for beating up egg whites, mayonnaise. But you can always do with more, so keep your eyes open.

Flan Tin: One 8 or 9 inch tin is essential. Better still, two, so you can bake two pastry cases at once, storing the extra one in an airtight tin.

Measuring Jug: I have a large plastic beaker which cost a few pence. It gives fluid oz., pint, sugar and flour measurement tables separately, and I find it invaluable. Kitchen scales are not so vital because exact measurements are less important with bulky dishes, but for pastry and cake making, where accuracy matters, the beaker is essential. (Butter and fat are simple – 2 oz. is a quarter of the packet, and so on.)

Implements: You will need an egg-whisk, two or three wooden spoons, a metal spatula for lifting fried foods, a coffee strainer and a grater. The last is essential for grating cheese, lemon rind, vegetables, and worth every penny it costs. Best are the four-sided plastic graters – stable and less painful on the knuckles.

When you can add to this basic selection, you should concentrate first on extra saucepans and casseroles. Other useful oddments are a loaf tin, good for baking Meat Loaf, Caramel Custards, cakes. A shallow ovenproof dish for baking fish and vegetables, or milk puddings. A garlic press. Chefs swat the bulb with a heavy chopper but, in less skilful hands, the fragments tend to fly round the room.

If you have an odd pound to spare any time, a Mouli food mill is the one gadget to invest in. Childishly simple to use, it takes the slog out of mushing soup, fruit and vegetables.

If you have no fridge look out for one of the old-fashioned butter coolers, still to be found in junk shops. They are made of porous earthenware, with a glass liner dish for the butter. You put a little water in the bottom and condensation keeps the butter firm but malleable, even in hot weather.

One last aid to cooking without tears. Free too! When making mayonnaise, put the oil in a corked bottle with a deep notch cut in one side of the cork. This regulates the flow of oil, greatly simplifying the task.

Weights and Measures

The most confusing feature of the whole gently anarchic weights and measures situation is the fact that there are two different ounce measurements in general use – the weight ounce and the fluid ounce – and unless one is on the alert this can lead to serious mistakes in measuring out the quantities for a recipe.

The point to grasp here is that a fluid ounce is the *volume* of an ounce *weight* of water. One pint equals 20 fl. oz. or $1\frac{1}{4}$ lb. of water. The standard British cup measure, as you will see if you check your measuring jug or beaker, holds 10 fl. oz. or half a pint of water or watery fluids like milk. So far so good. It is when converting weight measurements of solids like flour, sugar, breadcrumbs, rice, etc., into the volume terms of the standard cup measure, that you have to look sharp, because the weight/volume ratio is different in each case. In the case of flour and sugar the conversion is made easy because their respective weight equivalents are marked off on all standard measuring jugs. Thus you will see that flour is much lighter for its volume than water and that 10 oz. flour is almost double the volume of 10 fl. oz. or 1 cup water. Sugar, on the other hand, is almost as heavy for its volume as water, as you will see if you compare the 10 fl. oz. cup mark and the 10 oz. mark for sugar. Rice, conveniently, weighs almost exactly the same for its volume as sugar, and can be measured according to the same measure. Flour, sugar and rice are probably the substances most frequently measured in this way, but you might find the following table of approximate equivalents useful on occasion.

1 cup breadcrumbs	5 oz.
1 cup grated cheese	5 oz.
1 cup honey, treacle or syrup	15 oz.
1 cup oatmeal	8 oz.
1 cup nuts	5 oz.
1 cup dried fruit	8 oz.

1 tablespoon = half 1 fl. oz.

Getting to Know Your Oven

Ovens, particularly ovens attached to rather elderly cookers, do seem to vary quite a bit in efficiency. The older models, I find, seem to generate rather less heat. So what would be a moderate oven temperature on a brand-new cooker can be nearer to cool on an old one. Other factors like variations in the local gas pressure have to be taken into account, if you have a gas cooker. So don't accept temperature readings in the recipes in this book as final and irrevocable. They are as accurate a guide as possible, but if you find dishes consistently seem to take longer than the stated time to cook the chances are that your oven is a sluggish one and you should adjust the setting accordingly. Accuracy is not vitally important in the case of dishes needing long, slow cooking, at low-to-moderate temperatures, but where a dish calls for a hot oven it usually has to be hot or the dish may suffer. This is particularly true of pastry, soufflés, cakes and bread. If you have good reason to doubt the efficiency of your oven, step up the heat in these particular cases. Pre-heating the oven for a few minutes is a help too.

NOTE ON TEMPERATURES

In all recipes, I have given the regulo setting for gas ovens, and the Fahrenheit and Centigrade temperatures which most nearly correspond. (The number of degrees Centigrade is not always an exact conversion of the Fahrenheit temperature, but the variation is never more than a few degrees and is negligible for practical purposes.)

Standards

All the recipes in this chapter come into a category un-recognized, so far as I know, by cooking literature, but familiar to every reasonably experienced cook who usually makes his or her personal selection as time goes by. Quite simply, these are dishes which one can, and does, go back to, over and over again, with renewed pleasure and appetite. They extend over the whole field of eating – soups, salads, main dishes, puddings. They must taste good, certainly, in a homely rather than subtle fashion. They are often, though not always, easy to make successfully. Their components tend to be straightforward, and associative as well – pork and beans, frankfurters and red cabbage – which makes the shopping easier, especially from memory. They are, of course, thrifty, but without appearing stingy. Still, in the last resort, their appeal is elusive, and just why one should keep returning to these, after many promising alternatives have been discarded, is something of a mystery.

There is nothing mysterious, however, about my reason for

choosing to start my book with a whole collection of cooking Standards. I am convinced, from analysing my own experience and the food offered up regularly by friends, family and acquaintances, that these are the most useful recipes for an inperienced cook to start on, a good foundation on which to build a more elaborate repertoire as experience and confidence grow. Once you have mastered a selection of these recipes, you will be able to feed yourself and others cheaply, efficiently and well, and you will have picked up some useful knowledge along the way.

A few specific points

Soups: Ideal pauper's food – cheap, nourishing and good for you. If your experience is limited to tinned or packet varieties, you have no idea how good soup can be. A solid minestrone, with grated cheese, or a French onion soup poured over slices of bread, is almost a meal in itself. Certainly a light lunch. A lighter vegetable soup is, say, half a meal, and should be rounded out with a light main dish – grilled fish, pâté and salad, an omelette.

Main Dishes: Most in this chapter are substantial and need no more than one vegetable dish or salad as accompaniment. Many have their own stodge built in. Leftovers can be warmed up – indeed many of these dishes improve with keeping, within reason.

Puddings: Fresh fruit addicts probably won't bother with these. All the same it is worth learning up a few because they are useful when you have a lot of people to feed. Children love them, and so, oddly enough, do most men. A simple sweet like caramel custard or bread-and-butter pudding rounds off a skimpy meal pleasantly.

A guiding rule is that a meal can either be built round one solid dish, needing very little with, before or after, or a succession of light-weight dishes. The first is less trouble, the second offers more variety and is a better summer formula when salads and fruit are cheap and plentiful.

BASIC STOCK*

It is worth boiling up several pounds of bones at once, when making this stock, because the meaty jelly it produces will keep for several days, longer in the fridge, and can be used as the basis for a variety of substantial soups, as well as for enriching stews, braised meat and vegetable dishes, and any thick sauces for pasta. In fact, there are very few dishes using meat or vegetables which are not improved by a couple of spoons of stock mixed into them. A soup based on this stock is a meal by itself, eaten with bread and cheese.

Marrow bones, scraps of meat (optional), calf's foot or pig's trotter (optional), water

If you use a calf's foot or pig's trotter ask the butcher to split it for you. Put all the bones and any odd scraps of meat into a large saucepan, and cover with cold water. Bring to the boil slowly. Dramatic amounts of scum will rise as the water starts boiling. Skim these off with a large spoon. After a few minutes, the scum will have cleared. Reduce heat till the water is simmering gently, cover the pan and cook for 2 hours. Pour the liquid through a sieve into a large bowl and leave to cool. When cold, scrape off the thin layer of fat which will have formed on top of the jellied stock. The fat can be used for braising sausages, etc., so don't throw it away. You can also scoop the marrow out of your soup bones (while hot of course) and eat it on toast as a warming start to a cold meal.

N.B. This stock is intended to add richness and body rather than a pronounced flavour. Vegetables should not be added to basic stock because the jelly would then need to be boiled up daily to prevent it

31

going bad. It is better to leave it unseasoned too, because any subsequent reduction, i.e. boiling down, would make the seasoning too pronounced.

FRENCH ONION SOUP (*4 helpings*)

1 quart basic stock, 4 large or 6 small onions, knob of butter, ¼ lb. grated Cheddar, 4 slices toast, salt and pepper

Slice onions thickly, melt the butter in a heavy saucepan and fry onions over moderate heat till golden brown – not burnt. Stir from time to time to prevent them sticking. Pour in stock and bring to boil. Simmer for ½–¾ hour, covered. Taste and add salt and pepper. Toast four thick slices of bread, removing crusts if you are fussy. Grate cheese. Serve in individual bowls. Float a slice of toast on each serving and sprinkle generously with grated cheese.

ARTICHOKE SOUP* (*4 helpings*)

These are the Jerusalem artichokes, which look like small knobbly potatoes, not the leafy globe variety. Artichokes have a pronounced, though delicate, flavour, which makes a particularly good soup.

1 lb. Jerusalem artichokes, 1 oz. butter, 1½ pints water and 1 bouillon cube or stock, a little cream or top of milk, salt, pepper, nutmeg

Peel the artichokes, slice them and heat them gently in the butter for a few minutes. Add water and bouillon cube, or basic stock, to cover by about an inch, also salt, pepper and nutmeg, and simmer gently till tender – 45 minutes–1 hour. Sieve, return to pan and add a little cream or top of milk, or plain milk and butter.

If you have time, make some croûtons to eat with this. The small cubed sort are best, sprinkled over the soup.

CURRIED LENTIL SOUP* (*4–6 helpings*)

Good, strong, warming soup with a slight snap to it. Practically a meal on its own.

½ lb. lentils, 2 pints water or stock, 2 large onions, 1 turnip, 2 Tbs. butter, 2 tsp. curry powder, a little chutney juice, salt, pepper, a little flour

Fry the sliced onions and turnip in butter till soft. Sprinkle on curry powder and stir a few moments longer. Add the pre-soaked lentils and water or stock – if you are using water a bouillon cube will help, but go easy on the salt in that case. Simmer over low heat for 1½ hours or until the lentils can be squashed against the side of the pan with a spoon. Put the whole lot through a sieve or the Mouli. Return to the saucepan. Add salt and black pepper to taste, and the chutney juice. If the soup seems too thin, you can thicken it by mixing a little with 1 Tbs. flour, adding this to the soup and simmering, stirring from time to time, for another 10 minutes or so.

Eat this with slices of dry toast and butter.

HARICOT BEAN SOUP (*4–6 helpings*)

A good soup to make when you have some stock left from boiling a piece of bacon. Cooking the beans in this gives them a lot more flavour.

¾ lb. haricot beans, 3 pints stock, 1 onion, 1 clove garlic, 1 oz. butter, salt, pepper, 2 Tbs. chopped parsley, a little milk. A little chopped bacon, or fried croûtons as garnish

The beans should be soaked overnight. Skim any fat off the bacon stock, strain, and put in the beans, onion, garlic. Boil for 1–1½ hours, or until the beans are soft enough to crush easily with a wooden spoon. Put them through a sieve with the onion, garlic and liquor. Return to pan, stir well, add salt and pepper to taste, butter and a little milk if the soup seems too solid. It should be fairly thick. Stir in the parsley. Simmer a few minutes longer. If you have any chopped bacon, add this at the same time as the parsley.

Serve just as it is, or with little croûtons made of cubes of bread fried till golden in bacon fat, sprinkled over each serving.

In the absence of bacon stock, hot water plus the usual bouillon cubes (1 per pint) can be substituted.

CHESTNUT SOUP (*4–6 helpings*)

An elegant and original first course to serve at a mid winter supper party when chestnuts are cheap. It can be prepared ahead, and reheated and diluted with milk just before the meal.

1 lb. peeled chestnuts, 1 small onion, 1 stick celery, 2 pints chicken or other white stock, pinch sugar, salt and pepper, 1 tsp. grated lemon rind, whipping cream (optional), milk

Prepare chestnuts as for Mont Blanc (*see* p. 196). Then simmer them with the chopped onion and celery in the stock until they are soft enough to sieve. Now add the other seasonings and simmer for another ten minutes or so, till fairly smooth. Put through a sieve, or blend in the Mouli till smooth. If the mixture is very thick dilute it with milk. Reheat over low heat and serve with a blob of whipped cream.

MINESTRONE (*4–6 helpings*)

More a meal than a soup, this, and therefore economical, because only the greediest people would demand more than an omelette to follow. You can play about with the ingredients according to what is at hand – odd scraps of boiled bacon, a bacon bone, such vegetables as are cheap and in season, but keep to the rule of putting slow-cooking vegetables in ahead of the quicker cooking ones. And, of course, using stock (*see* p. 31) instead of water and bouillon cubes gives a much richer soup.

Suggested ingredients: 3 pints stock, $\frac{1}{4}$ lb. haricot beans (soaked overnight), $\frac{1}{4}$ lb. belly of pork *or* bacon bones *or* a few rashers of bacon, 3 carrots, 3 onions, 2–3 potatoes, a turnip, $\frac{1}{2}$ small cabbage, 3 cloves garlic, herbs, tomato purée, a handful of macaroni, salt, pepper, grated cheese

Prepare all the vegetables, in other words, peel and slice them. Heat up the stock separately. In your soup pan (which had better be a big one) heat a spoonful of oil. In this, gently fry cut-up pieces of belly of pork (rind removed), or bits of bacon and the sliced onions and garlic, stirring to make sure nothing burns. Now add the hot stock, drained haricot beans, 1 bayleaf, pinch thyme and marjoram and a generous helping of tomato purée. A small tin of peeled tomatoes can be substituted here. Boil at a moderate pace for $1\frac{1}{2}$–2 hours, or until the beans are tender. Now add sliced carrots, turnip, potatoes. Ten minutes later put in sliced cabbage, leeks (if you are using them), and the handful of macaroni. After a further 10 minutes, taste, and add salt and pepper as needed.

Serve this up with a bowl of grated cheese so everyone can help themselves, and large slices of bread and butter.

Other vegetables which can go in include celery, beans, peas, a Jerusalem artichoke or two, even a few spring greens, well trimmed.

BORSHCH (*4–6 helpings*)

Borshch is to Russia what Scotch Broth is to Scotland. It is a cheering soup to look at, ruby red, and the beetroot and sour cream give it an interesting acidulated sweetness.

1 quart basic stock, 1 lb. uncooked beetroots, 1 onion, 1 carrot, $\frac{1}{4}$ pint sour cream *or* thin cream and a little lemon juice, salt and pepper to taste

Peel and dice beetroots into smallish pieces. Chop onion and carrot roughly. Add vegetables to stock and bring to boil. Reduce heat, cover and simmer 1–2 hours, or until the beetroot is very pale and the soup very red. Add salt and pepper to taste. The Russian way would be to strain off the vegetables, but if you prefer a thicker soup you could sieve them and return them to the pan. A spoonful of cream – soured with a squeeze of lemon juice – is added to each helping of soup.

If you have any pickled beetroot, 1 Tbs. of the juice can be added to the borshch. The soup can be made equally successfully with chicken stock.

SCOTS FISH SOUP* (*4 helpings*)

Cullen Skink is the traditional name for this soup. The Scots use Finnan haddock but any cheap white fish will do – cod fillet, whiting, bream. Those living on the east coast may be able to get hold of a cod's head, which is the cheapest thing out. Otherwise, any fish bones and heads you can wheedle out of the fishmonger will enrich the soup.

$\frac{1}{2}$ lb. fish, odd bones, etc., 1 onion, $\frac{1}{2}$–1 pint milk, 1 large potato, nutmeg, butter, salt, pepper

Chop the onion coarsely, peel and cut up the potato. Melt 1 oz. butter in a large saucepan over gentle heat. Put in the vegetables and stir them about till they have soaked up most of butter and the onions are getting soft. Put in the fish, bones, etc., and about 1 pint of water. Bring to the boil and simmer for 1 hour. Pick out bones and skin, and put the remainder through a sieve. Return to the pan, add milk till the soup has the consistency you like. Season with salt, pepper, a liberal sprinkling of grated nutmeg. Simmer for another ten minutes. Just before serving add a lump of butter and stir it in.

Fried croûtons, little triangles of bread fried crisp in butter, offset the blandness of this soup. I think a handful of grated cheese mixed in is an improvement too, as it is with many fish dishes.

FRENCH DRESSING

The most commonly used dressing for both cooked and raw salads, this is composed, in its classic state, of nothing but oil, vinegar, salt and pepper. Three parts oil, to one part vinegar, a good pinch of salt and pepper to taste.

Unless you are using the best quality ingredients however – French wine vinegar, fine olive oil – the dressing will almost certainly be improved by adding various other flavourings. The choice is huge and there is nothing to stop you working out your own formula. But the usual garlic and mustard one, with or without chopped fresh herbs, is hard to beat. In this case you can use 1 crushed garlic clove and 1 tsp. French mustard (or a pinch of dry mustard) with the basic oil/vinegar mixture, and as many chopped herbs – chives, tarragon, parsley, thyme, chervil, basil are a few often used – as you like. A tsp. of sugar is an improvement if you are using malt vinegar and dry mustard. If you like a suggestion of garlic more than the actual bulb, rub a cut clove round the salad bowl, or on a crust of stale bread, sprinkled with a few drops of oil, which you bury at the bottom of the salad, to exhale, as the French writers lyrically put it, its incomparable fragrance.

You can mix up the dressing in the salad bowl itself, stirring the various ingredients into the oil before adding the vinegar and chopped herbs. Or, more economically, you can shake it up in a bottle. Whichever way, make sure the ingredients are well mixed before dressing the salad, and toss the salad about with a couple of spoons (less fastidious people can use their fingers) till it is all well coated. Once dressed, try not to leave the salad standing too long – this applies to lettuce, cress, chicory and curly endive in particular – or it will begin to go flabby and the oil and vinegar will separate.

Other ingredients which turn up in salad dressings include grated orange rind, crumbled blue cheese (an American fad this), a whole range of fancy vinegars – cider, tarragon, garlic – honey, nuts, sultanas, white wine, tabasco, Worcestershire Sauce, lemon juice, sieved hard-boiled egg yolk, pounded anchovies. Also more exotic herbs like fennel and dill. There is no harm in experimenting a little, though I would not advise trying them all out at once.

MAYONNAISE

Mayonnaise seems to share with soufflés an undeserved reputation for being unpredictable as an operatic diva. I can't really see it myself. It can, and occasionally does, curdle, for no very clear reason, but it can almost always be rescued by starting again with a fresh egg yolk and beating in the curdled substance little by little. Make sure all the ingredients are at room temperature. Remove eggs from fridge or cool larder well in advance. It is also a good idea to pre-heat the jug for the oil by rinsing with boiling water, then drying, before filling with oil.

For a smallish quantity of mayonnaise allow one egg yolk to approximately $\frac{1}{2}$ pint of olive oil. *Do* use real olive oil. The flavour of the oil is the whole point of the sauce.

To make it you need a bowl, a wooden spoon, a small jug for the oil, a little dry mustard, salt and pepper to mix in to the egg yolk, and a little vinegar or a squeeze of lemon juice to finish off with.

Break the yolk into the bowl. Stir well with your spoon, blending in the dry ingredients till smooth. Now start adding the oil, a drop or two at a time, stirring between each addition. After a minute or so the mixture in the bowl should be getting the smooth, shiny look and firm consistency of a successful oil-and-egg-yolk emulsion, which is what a mayonnaise is. When it gets to this stage you can step up the oil doses a little – a drip instead of a drop, but make sure you stir it in thoroughly before adding more. By the time you have used up more than half the oil you can increase this to a small splash. When your oil allowance is gone, you should have a firm pale yellow substance, rather similar to a packet custard in consistency. A squeeze of lemon juice or a dash of vinegar stirred in rapidly will thin it down. If it still seems too firm you can add more oil, or a little boiling water – 1 Tbs. – to lighten it, though personally I think a rather solid mayonnaise has more pungency. The sauce is now ready to be mixed into salads, or used to coat hard-boiled eggs, cold fish, chicken, and so forth.

When your mayonnaise curdles, you will be confronted by a queasy mixture with a runny texture which refuses to jell as a mayonnaise should. If you are in any doubt, leave the mixture to stand for a few minutes – if it *has* curdled, or separated, one look will confirm the fact. What you do now is break another egg yolk, into a fresh bowl, add the usual ingredients, stir in oil, drop by drop, till firm and only then add your curdled mixture, little by little, alternating with oil. The only snag to this is that you will need to use more oil to get the consistency right, so you will have more mayonnaise at the end. The surplus can be stored for a few days in a glass jar with a screw top.

Basic mayonnaise can be converted into various other classic sauces by adding certain ingredients. Sauce Remoulade, for instance, a sharp sauce which is delicious with grilled meat, is mayonnaise ($\frac{1}{2}$ pint) with rather more mustard added (2 tsp.), plus some chopped gherkins and capers, a dash of Anchovy Essence and a spoonful of chopped herbs, in this case parsley, tarragon and chervil. (If you can't get them all never mind.)

The celebrated Sauce Tartare, which is excellent with rather fattier, fried food (fish, chops, etc.), has 1 hard-boiled egg yolk worked into the raw egg yolk before proceeding as for mayonnaise. At the end, add rather more vinegar – 1 Tbs. – and chopped gherkins, capers and herbs as for Remoulade, plus the chopped white of the hard-boiled egg.

A recipe for garlic mayonnaise, or aïoli, follows.

AÏOLI

Aïoli is a mayonnaise powerfully flavoured with garlic. In Provence, where it comes from, they eat it with plainly boiled fish or beef and an assortment of vegetables – carrots, beans, potatoes – also boiled and usually hot. It also goes well with hard-boiled eggs, and boiled chicken. If you like garlic you will probably find yourself thinking up excuses for eating aïoli.

Start by squeezing or pounding two or three cloves of garlic (2 cloves, 1 egg yolk and $\frac{1}{3}$ pint of oil is about right for 2 people) to a pulp. Then stir in the egg yolk, and add the oil drop by drop to start with, beating all the time with a wooden spoon. When it starts to thicken, you can add the oil in slightly larger quantities. The procedure, in other words is exactly as for mayonnaise. (*See* p. 39 for what to do if it should curdle.) When you have made as much as you need add a squeeze of lemon juice and a little salt and stir again.

Try this with boiled cod steaks, and an assortment of the vegetables above.

MUSTARD SAUCE

This is a quickly made and highly pungent sauce traditionally served with grilled herrings and rabbit. It also goes well with sausages, or any dull bit of meat you want to add some excitement to.

1 oz. butter, ½ Tbs. flour, 1 tsp. vinegar, salt, pepper, 1 Tbs. dry mustard and approximately ¼ pint water

Melt the butter in a double saucepan, stir in all the other ingredients and keep stirring vigorously till smooth and thick. If the sauce seems too thick, add more water. A few capers can be put in for extra punch.

BREAD SAUCE*

Bread sauce and Cumberland Sauce are Britain's most distinguished creations in the sauce line. Even the French, who like to damn our cooking with the faintest of praise, are impressed by these two. Bread sauce, as you doubtless know, is eaten with roast chicken. Even if you don't have roast chicken very often it is worth knowing about because it is easily made and always popular.

1 medium onion, 2 cloves, 1 bayleaf, ½ pint milk, salt, pepper, a little butter, 3–4 heaped Tbs. fresh white breadcrumbs

Stick the cloves into the onion and put this and the bayleaf with the milk into a saucepan. Cover and set on a very low heat till the milk is well flavoured – 10 minutes will do, but nearer 20 is better. Then take out the onion and bayleaf, stir in the crumbs – grated from a white loaf – and simmer for a few minutes till the sauce is thick but not stodgy. Now add salt, pepper and a little butter (or cream if you have any to spare). Heat through and serve.

TOMATO SAUCE

You can use fresh tomatoes, peeled tinned tomatoes, a mixture of peeled tinned tomatoes and tomato purée, or, at a pinch, purée alone but the latter will need padding out with extra onion, and possibly a little carrot, to make up the necessary bulk.

For two people as a sauce for pasta, 1 lb. tomatoes or a medium-sized tin of peeled tomatoes, will be enough. With this you will need 1 clove garlic, 1 chopped onion, a couple of bacon rashers (or the remains of a meat stew), sugar, salt and pepper to taste, and if possible a little fresh or dried basil, or failing that, a bayleaf

Quarter fresh tomatoes, chop the garlic finely and cut the bacon into thin strips. Put all the ingredients – if you are using purée alone make it up to the amount you want with water or stock and add some more chopped onion and a sliced carrot – into a pan, cover, and leave to simmer very gently till it has reduced somewhat and most of the liquid has evaporated. Put the sauce through a sieve, return to the pan to heat up for a moment, and if you like, stir a little butter in before serving.

To make a much meatier sauce, more of a Bolognese than Neapolitan, use the same ingredients plus $\frac{1}{4}-\frac{1}{2}$ lb. beef mince. I find it has more flavour and the mince is less gritty if cooked like this.

Fry bacon snippets and chopped onion and garlic gently in a little oil or butter. Add mince, and stir it about till lightly browned. Cook for a minute or two, then add the tomatoes and other ingredients, season strongly, transfer the lot to a small casserole (preferably earthenware), cover, and finish cooking in a low oven (Gas 3, 325°F., 150°C.) for $1\frac{1}{2}-2$ hours, or until the sauce looks thick and appetizing.

Any beef marrow, meat stock or meaty leftovers can be added to this last sauce.

BASIC WHITE SAUCE

Basic white sauce, like basic stock, is a neutral-tasting compound which absorbs the flavours you add to it. I don't think there is much to be said for the practice of pouring it over boiled vegetables to make them look more genteel. But as a binding for certain casserole dishes – fish pie, onion-bacon-and-potato hotpot – and as a base for cheese and onion sauces, it is extremely useful. A thick white sauce is also the foundation for most soufflés.

For some reason the making of this sauce is surrounded with complications in most cookbooks. The milk, they tell you, should be heated separately, added little by little to the flour-and-butter mixture, and the whole preparation needs constant stirring to prevent lumps or burning. The method suggested here, which was given to me by a wise and experienced cook, is beautifully simple, uses only one pan, and you don't even need to stir – though I must admit I usually do once or twice to be on the safe side. The whole operation only takes three or four minutes.

For one pint of white sauce you will need 1 pint milk, 1 rounded Tbs. butter and 1 rounded Tbs. flour

Melt the butter in a saucepan over moderate heat, stir in the flour thoroughly, pour in the pint of milk (cold), increase heat and bring fairly rapidly to the boil. I usually give it a stir at this point to make sure it is not sticking to the bottom of the pan, though if you don't cook it over fierce heat it shouldn't do so. In a few minutes it will have thickened to the right consistency. If there are any lumps you can disperse them with a few turns of the egg beater.

If you are using the white sauce as a base for cheese or onion sauce, you should simmer it gently for a while to get rid of the taste of the flour. Twenty minutes, over an asbestos mat, would be ideal, but ten minutes is adequate. If it is to be used in a dish which requires further cooking anyway, like fish pie, you can dispense with the extra simmering and it will be ready as soon as it has thickened.

EGGS IN ONION SAUCE* (*Main meal for 2, or first course for 4*)

5–6 eggs, 1 pint milk, 1 Tbs. flour, 2 Tbs. butter, ½ lb. onions, nutmeg, salt, pepper, fried bread

The number of eggs depends on how hungry you are. This is usually classified as a light meal, but the sauce makes it surprisingly filling. The eggs should be what the French call 'mollets', that is, cooked till the whites are firm and the yolks still creamy.

First, get the sauce under way. Slice and chop the onions and soften them in 1 Tbs. butter, over moderate heat, stirring occasionally. They should be stewed in the butter rather than fried. Now melt 1 rounded Tbs. butter in another pan and stir in 1 rounded Tbs. flour. Pour on 1 pint milk and leave to come to the boil and thicken, over moderate heat. Put on a pan of water for the eggs. Lower them in just before it boils (this helps to reduce the risk of cracking) and cook for just over 5 minutes. Pour off the boiling water, run cold water over them for a minute and set aside. By now the onions should be softening to a mush. Add a little more butter if they show any signs of sticking. Reduce heat under the sauce, which should now be thick, to simmering point. Put the onions through a sieve with a wooden spoon and add the resulting purée to the sauce. Season the sauce with salt, pepper and nutmeg to taste and leave it to cook gently, while you peel the eggs and fry the bread croûtons which go well with this dish.

Cut the peeled eggs in half and arrange them in a shallow fireproof dish. If you haven't got one, use a flan tin. Take crusts off four thin slices of bread, cut them across into triangles and fry in a little butter till crisp, turning and pressing them into the hot butter. Now pour the sauce over the eggs and put them under the grill for 2 or 3 minutes, till the sauce is lightly browned. Arrange the croûtons round the dish and serve.

BACON AND EGG FLAN* (*2–4 helpings*)

This is a dish which looks as good as it tastes. An adaptation of the French Quiche Lorraine, it is an open flan filled with a firm cheese-and-onion flavoured savoury custard, studded with snippets of bacon and tomato rings. It is one of the cheapest recipes in this book, and one of the quickest and easiest, especially if you have a pre-baked flan case (*see* 'blind' cooked pastry, p. 102) ready to take the filling. It tastes equally good hot, tepid (as the French eat it) or cold. One flan is a substantial meal for two, or a first course for four people.

Short pastry flan case (7 or 8 in.), 1 egg and 1 yolk, 1–2 oz. grated Cheddar, ⅓ pint milk or top of milk, 1 small onion, 1 tomato, 2 oz. bacon, salt and pepper, nutmeg (optional), butter

For short pastry instructions *see* p. 100. To make the filling, beat eggs and grated cheese together in a bowl, adding milk, salt and pepper, and a dash of grated nutmeg if you like the flavour. Cut bacon into snippets, chop the onion finely and fry both in a little butter till they begin to change colour – the onion should be softening and the bacon hardening. Then arrange the bacon and onion in the flan case, stick tomato slices here and there and pour over the egg mixture. Bake in a moderate oven (gas 5, 370°F., 190°C.) till firm and golden brown, between 45 minutes and 1 hour.

All you need with this is a dressed green salad.

MUSHROOM FLAN (*3–4 helpings*)

A pleasant flan with a particularly rich-tasting filling. The quantities given would make a first course for four or a light supper dish for three, served with a crisp salad like chicory dressed with lemon juice and olive oil.

Short crust pastry flan case, 6 oz. mushrooms, 1 small onion.

1½ oz. butter, 1 Tbs. flour, ½ pint milk, pinch of mace, 1 egg yolk, 1 Tbs. grated cheese or 2 Tbs. cream, salt, pepper

Chop the onion roughly. Melt some of the butter in a small pan and gently fry the onion in it till soft and golden. Remove from heat and stir in the flour. Meanwhile bring the milk, seasoned with salt, pepper and mace, to the boil and pour over the onion and flour, mixing thoroughly. Return to heat and leave to simmer gently for a few minutes while you prepare the mushrooms. Break the mushrooms into pieces, and chop the stalks roughly. Fry in a little butter till soft – about three minutes. Mix the mushrooms into the milk and onion mixture. Remove from heat. Leave to cool for a few minutes, then stir in the beaten egg yolk and cream or grated cheese. Fill the flan case with the mixture. Bake in a hot oven (gas 7, 425°F., 220°C.) for 20 minutes, then reduce heat (gas 5, 375°F., 190°C.) and cook for another 15–20 minutes, or until the pastry is lightly browned and the filling firm and set.

KEDGEREE* (4 helpings)

Originally an Anglo-Indian breakfast dish, in the days when breakfast was a solid meal, kedgeree now turns up regularly as a main course in most of the pauper households I know. If you haven't come across it before, it is worth trying. It is cheap, tasty, and very simple to make.

½ lb. smoked haddock, ¾ lb. rice, 3 hard-boiled eggs, 3 onions, salt, pepper, butter

Put the haddock in a baking tin with a little water, or milk and water, cover with a piece of buttered paper (the wrapping off a butter pat is useful for this) and bake in a moderate oven (gas 4, 350°F., 180°C.) for 20 minutes or until the fish comes off the skin easily. Drain, remove any skin and bone, and flake. Boil rice for 12 minutes in plenty of salted water, drain, rinse with hot water under the tap for a minute and return to pan. Cover the pan and leave the rice to dry off for a few minutes over lowest possible heat. Slice the onions, chop roughly and fry in butter over moderate heat till they are soft and golden-brown. The rice should now be dry, the grains separate. Stir in 2–3 oz. butter (butter is the making of this dish so don't skimp), salt and pepper. Add onions, sliced hard-boiled eggs and fish. Stir it all together lightly with a fork, add a little more butter if you think it can do with it and serve. Tomato ketchup goes well with kedgeree. Or a squeeze of lemon juice.

You can vary the basic dish in many ways. Some people add raisins or sultanas. You can stir in cream and a good pinch of curry powder, as they did under the Raj. The fish need not be smoked haddock; other cooked flaked white fish may be substituted – salt or fresh cod, even kippers if you can be bothered with de-boning them.

COD CAKE* (*4 generous helpings*)

An old-fashioned American dish, really a giant fish cake. A useful way of using up leftover white fish and cold potatoes.

½ lb. cooked cod, ½ lb. cold boiled potatoes, 1 cup dry bread-crumbs, 1 small onion minced very fine, salt, pepper, pinch of mace or nutmeg, 3 oz. butter, 2 eggs

If you are not using leftovers you will have first to cook the cod and boil the potatoes. Salt the cod, dot with butter, pour a little water around and bake in the oven covered with grease-proof paper or foil, for 20 minutes (gas 4, 350°F., 180°C.). When cod and potatoes have cooled enough to handle, flake the fish, removing skin and bones, and dice the potatoes. Mix with half the cupful of breadcrumbs. Stir in 2 egg whites and season with salt, pepper, mace or nutmeg, and finely minced onion. Whisk up egg yolks. Shape the fish mixture into a flat round cake, brush with egg yolk and roll in remaining crumbs. Melt a little butter in the frying pan and fry the cake light brown on both sides. Lower heat and let it continue cooking over moderate heat for 7–10 minutes longer. If it shows signs of burning add a little water.

Serve with a plain green vegetable and fresh or bottled tomato sauce.

FISH PIE* (*2 helpings*)

There are dozens of more or less elaborate versions of fish pie. To my mind the simple, classic version given here, combining fish, hard-boiled egg in a creamy and faintly cheesy white sauce, is the best of all. The preparation and cooking should be done with care.

Any firm white fish can be used: cod, bream, bass. Coley, if you can get it, is an excellent cheap substitute for cod, with a dark meat which turns white when cooked, and a good flavour. For economy's sake you can omit the shrimps.

½ lb. white fish, 2 oz. shrimps, ½ pint thick white sauce, 2 hard-boiled eggs, 2 oz. grated cheese, ½ tsp. dry mustard, salt and pepper, dried breadcrumbs or mashed potato.

First bake the fish in a little water, to which you can add a bayleaf, in a moderate oven. This should take between 20 and 30 minutes. Drain the fish on to a plate, reserving the cooking water, remove any skin and bones and divide into chunks.

Make the white sauce as for Basic White Sauce (*see* p. 42) by melting 1 oz. butter in a pan and adding 1 oz. flour and the fish stock made up to ½ pint with milk and stirring till thick. Salt and pepper to taste, add cheese and mustard and simmer for a few minutes. Remove from heat and stir in fish, shrimps and chopped hard-boiled egg. Turn into oven dish. Either sprinkle the top with breadcrumbs, or spread a layer of mashed potatoes over it, dot with butter and bake in a moderate oven (gas 4, 350°F., 180°C.) till the top is brown.

Baked tomatoes (*see* p. 68) go nicely with this.

STUFFED HERRINGS (*4 helpings*)

4 large herrings, 1 small onion or shallot, parsley, dill (optional), 2 oz. butter, salt and pepper

Choose herrings with soft roes. Chop onion or shallot and parsley very finely with the roes. Stir in melted butter, salt and pepper. Stuff the herrings with this mixture, wrap them in foil or oiled paper and put in the oven (gas 6, 400°F., 205°C.) for half an hour.

These are good eaten with plenty of French mustard and mashed potatoes.

HERRINGS BOULANGÈRE* (*4 helpings*)

A classic but unpretentious French method of cooking these cheap, excellent fish. You need 1 large or 2 small herrings per person. Ask the fishmonger to clean them without splitting them.

4 large or 8 small herrings, 1 large potato, 1 large onion, thyme, powdered bayleaf, salt, pepper, 3 oz. butter

Butter generously a flat shallow oven dish (a roasting pan would be quite suitable). Lay the herrings in a row down the middle. Sprinkle them with a little salt and pepper, and a pinch of thyme and powdered bayleaf. Peel and slice the potato very thinly indeed, likewise the onion, which should also be roughly chopped to speed the cooking. Arrange the sliced potato and chopped onion round the fish. Melt 3 oz. butter in a small pan and pour over the fish and vegetables. Add enough cold water barely to cover the fish. Bring the water to the boil on top of the stove (use an asbestos mat to be on the safe side). Then transfer the pan or dish to a fairly hot oven (gas 5, 375°F., 200°C.) and leave, basting with the liquid from the pan occasionally, till the vegetables are tender and the fish cooked. Approximately 45 minutes.

The vegetables cooked with the fish are more of a garnish than a substantial vegetable accompaniment. The French tend to prefer their fish dishes to consist mainly of fish. English tastes can be catered for by boiling up more potatoes separately, plus a green vegetable like kale, which goes particularly well with herrings.

MACKEREL FILLETS LYONNAISE★ (2 helpings)

Onions are the characteristic ingredient of dishes from the French town of Lyons, which is celebrated for its robust, highly flavoured cooking. They combine particularly well with mackerel, a strong-tasting fish in its own right.

2 large or 4 small mackerel, filleted, 2 large or 3 medium onions, 2 Tbs. white wine vinegar, 2 oz. butter, salt, pepper, dried breadcrumbs, 2–3 Tbs. cider, white wine or water

Peel and slice the onions thinly. Melt 1½ oz. butter in pan over low heat, add the onions, cover, and stew very gently till soft, stirring from time to time. Now moisten the onion with 2 Tbs. vinegar – if you have to use malt vinegar, 1 Tbs. will be enough, as it has a much stronger flavour. Spread half the onion on the bottom of a flat ovenproof dish. Season the mackerel fillets with salt and pepper, and lay them on top of the onions. Cover with the remaining onions. Pour the cider, wine or plain water over the top. Sprinkle with breadcrumbs and dot with butter. Bake in a fairly hot oven (gas 5, 375°F., 200°C.) for 20–30 minutes, or until the fillets are cooked. They will be firm and flaky when prodded with a fork.

Serve with buttered, baked potatoes and spinach or kale.

SWEDISH SMOKED FISH PUDDING (*2 helpings*)

The Scandinavians ring countless changes on the theme of fish and potatoes. To vary this, which is simple but tasty, try using a tin of brisling or sild (drained of oil) instead of the smoked fish. A little sour cream stirred with the eggs, makes it richer.

1 golden cutlet, or $\frac{1}{2}$ lb. smoked haddock, 4 medium-sized potatoes, 2 eggs, salt, black pepper, a little milk or cream

Pour boiling water over fish in a dish, leave for a minute, then drain, and flake fish, removing any bone, skin, etc. Peel, thinly slice the potatoes, wash the slices in a colander to remove starch and pat dry. Butter a fireproof dish, layer fish and potato slices alternately, ending up with a layer of overlapping potato slices. Whisk up eggs with salt, black pepper and about $\frac{1}{4}$ pint of milk or cream. Pour over the dish, and bake in a moderate oven (gas 5, 375°F., 200°C.) for about forty-five minutes, till the top is golden brown.

MUSSELS AND SPAGHETTI* (*2 helpings*)

There are depressing reports that mussels are becoming increasingly prized and expensive on the Continent, but for the moment they are still outstandingly good value for money. This recipe is one I evolved over many years of mussel eating – it is quick, easy and delicious. The combination of shellfish and pasta may sound incongruous, but it is very good – it was suggested by an Italian dish made with spaghetti and clams.

1 quart mussels, 1 onion, 1 clove garlic, 1 small tin peeled tomatoes or 1 Tbs. tomato purée, $\frac{1}{2}$ tsp. Vindaloo paste, 1 tsp. vinegar or lemon juice, thyme, olive oil, spaghetti

Chop onion and garlic finely and soften in a little oil in a deep heavy pan. When soft, add the peeled tomatoes or purée, the Vindaloo paste, lemon juice or vinegar and thyme. Cook gently for about 10 minutes until you have a soft mush. If the mixture gets too dry, add a little water. Not too much, because the mussels release their own juice.

Meanwhile have a large pan of salted water boiling for the spaghetti. Half a packet should be enough for two. Boil hard for about 12 minutes, till tender but not sticky. (A little oil in the water helps stop the pan boiling over.) Drain and return to the pan with a knob of butter, and pepper.

The mussels should have been well scraped, and the beards pulled off. Discard any which don't close. Wash through with running water in a colander to remove sand.

Turn up the heat under the pan with the tomato mixture and put in the mussels. Cover, and leave for 2 or 3 minutes. The mussels are ready as soon as they have all opened.

Serve a large mound of spaghetti on each plate with a ladle of mussels and the sauce on top. You will need a bowl to take the discarded shells.

SWEDISH MEAT BALLS (*2 helpings*)

The chopped capers and pickled beet give these little rissoles an interesting, slightly tart flavour.

½ lb. minced beef, 1 dessertspoon capers, 1 dessertspoon pickled beetroot, 1 small onion, 1 pinch of dill (optional), a dash of Worcestershire Sauce, 1 Tbs. grated stale white bread

Chop the capers and pickled beet together. Chop the onion very finely with a sharp knife. Soak the crumbs in a little water and squeeze dry. Combine all the ingredients, mixing well with a knife or your hands. Leave them to stand for an hour or so, if possible, so that the flavours mix. Then shape into small flat patties. You can either flour both sides and fry in a little oil over a moderate flame for 10–15 minutes, or – which is easier on the digestion – put the rissoles in an ovenproof dish with a little butter and a piece of buttered paper over them and bake (gas 6, 400°F., 205°C.) for ½–¾ hour, until they are cooked through.

The only problem with these rissoles is knowing when they are done, because the beetroot gives them a deep pink colour quite unlike the usual appearance of cooked beef. The only test is to taste one.

They are good served with mashed potatoes and buttered greens of spinach.

CURRIED MEAT BALLS (*4 helpings*)

¾ lb. beef mince, 3–4 Tbs. soft breadcrumbs, 1 finely chopped onion, 1 chopped clove garlic, salt, 1 tsp. Vindaloo paste or 1 dessertspoon curry powder, 1 egg, lemon juice, flour, oil and butter for frying

Mix all the ingredients well and leave them to stand for an hour or two to develop the flavours. To make the meat balls scoop up a spoonful of the mixture at a time, pat it into a small round cake, dust it with flour on both sides (you need enough flour to stop it feeling sticky) and fry in a mixture of oil and butter over moderate heat till brown on both sides, turning with a spatula from time to time. As the cakes are finished transfer them to a plate in a low oven. Before serving, squeeze a little lemon juice over them.

Eat with baked potatoes and a green salad.

This recipe was suggested to me by my butcher. Like all mince recipes, it is best made with a piece of lean stewing steak freshly minced up for you, but thanks to the camouflaging properties of the Vindaloo paste/curry powder it is also an effective disguise for indifferent ready-ground mince.

HOUGH* (8–10 helpings)

Hough is the traditional Scots version of brawn, or 'potted head'. The original recipe calls for an ox head, but as these are (a) hard to come by, and (b) fearsomely large, I substitute a mixture of ox cheek and shin which works quite well.

1 lb. ox cheek, 1 lb. shin of beef, 1 calf's foot (or pig's trotter, or veal knuckle) for the gelatine, 1 large onion, 1 carrot, mace, 1 clove, cayenne (optional), 1 bayleaf, salt, pepper, mustard

Ask the butcher to chop the foot/trotter/knuckle into three pieces for you. Wash it carefully. Put all the meats into a large saucepan with water to cover and bring to the boil. Skim off the scum which will rise for the first few minutes. When the water is bubbling fairly clear add sliced onion and carrot, bayleaf, mace (small pinch or blade), clove, a little salt and pepper, and simmer the whole lot gently for 3 hours.

Take out all the meat and chop off the best bits, discarding bones, gristle, fat, and cut it up fairly small. Meanwhile boil up the stock rapidly, to reduce and thicken it, adding a pinch of mustard and cayenne. Put the chopped meat into a wetted bowl, strain the stock through a sieve, and pour over the meat. Lay a plate on top with a weight on it and leave the hough overnight.

Next day scrape off any fat which has risen to the top, and turn out the hough.

This should be eaten with salad, baked potatoes and lots of mustard. If you have any wine to spare (ends of bottles which have gone slightly sour) you can make a more glamorous version of hough, by adding it to the water you cook it in, plus a couple of cloves of chopped garlic.

BRAIN FRITTERS* (*2 helpings*)

Brains are a taste worth cultivating, because a pair of calf or ox brains are very cheap indeed, and though they are a little fussy to prepare, the flavour is delicate and brains are nourishing and easily digested. Brain fritters like these figure in the Italian Fritto Misto.

1 pair calf or ox brains, 1 onion, sprig parsley, 1 bayleaf, 1 tsp. vinegar, salt, pepper

Fritter Batter: ¼ lb. flour, 3 Tbs. olive oil, pinch salt, ¼ pint tepid water, 1 stiffly beaten egg white

The batter should be prepared first (*see* Normandy Apple Fritter recipe, p. 110) and left to stand for 2 hours or longer, the beaten egg white being added just before frying.

The brains should be soaked in tepid water with a little vinegar for an hour or so. The water should be changed from time to time, and any little clots of blood adhering to the brains carefully removed – brains need gentle handling or they are apt to disintegrate. When the soaking water looks clear heat 1 pint water with 1 chopped onion, parsley, bayleaf, 1 tsp. vinegar, salt and pepper. When this is simmering gently, lower brains into the water and simmer for ½ hour. Remove, drain and leave to cool.

To cook the fritters heat a lot of oil in a deep frying pan. Divide the brains into pieces about the size of a walnut, dip them into the batter and then drop into the hot oil. They are cooked when they float to the top, about 3 minutes. Drain on kitchen paper. Eat with a squeeze of lemon juice.

BRAISED HEARTS (*2 helpings*)

2 sheep hearts, 1 large onion, 1 handful chopped sage (1 Tbs. dried), 2 Tbs. fresh breadcrumbs, flour, 2 oz. butter, 3 chopped and skinned tomatoes, 1 bayleaf, a little stock or water

Wash hearts well and cut out the gristle in the middle and the large vein, with a pair of scissors. Chop onion very fine and mix with the breadcrumbs, sage and a little butter. Push stuffing into wide hole at the top of the hearts and sew up the edges with a large needle and thick cotton – a thimble helps, as the needle gets very slippery. Roll the hearts in a little flour, brown lightly in butter or dripping in a small casserole. Add a little water or stock, stirring to mix it with the brown deposit on the bottom of the pan. Add the chopped peeled tomatoes, salt, pepper, the bayleaf, and cook in a moderate oven (gas 3, 300°F., 150°C.), covered, for at least 2 hours.

Serve with boiled potatoes or rice and buttered carrots or any green vegetable except cabbage.

OXTAIL STEW (*4–6 helpings*)

Oxtail makes a rich, thick stew with a good meaty flavour. The pieces of tail should be washed, dipped in boiling water and dried before frying with the onions.

1 medium-sized oxtail, jointed, 2 onions, 2 carrots, 1 stalk celery, 1 turnip, 2 cloves, pinch of mace, 1 Tbs. flour, juice of half a lemon, salt, pepper, butter

Separate the jointed pieces of oxtail. Wash them, dip them in boiling water for a minute, and then dry them carefully. Roll the pieces in flour, seasoned with salt and pepper. Melt 1 oz. butter in a heavy casserole, and put in the pieces of meat and sliced onions when it is sizzling. Turn them over so that the meat browns on all sides. Add the other cleaned, sliced vegetables, the cloves, mace and enough water to cover the lot. Bring the pot to the boil, skimming off any froth which rises to the top. Reduce heat to simmering point, cover the pot with a piece of foil or greaseproof paper and the lid. Simmer very slowly for 3 hours or longer, if you are not in a hurry. The meat should be falling off the bone. Taste the stock and add salt and pepper, if needed. Should you feel up to it, the appearance of the dish will be improved if you pick out the pieces of meat and put the stock and vegetables through a sieve, returning the thickened stock and meat to the pot for a few minutes to heat up again. Either way squeeze in the juice of half a lemon just before serving.

Plainly cooked, homely vegetables go best with oxtail – boiled potatoes, carrots, cabbage.

LIVER IN THE VENETIAN MANNER* (2 *helpings*)

Fried liver and onions is a well-known combination. The Venetian way of preparing it is the nicest of all, the onions stewed very slowly and gently in a little oil with the liver – cut into small thin strips – stirred in towards the end.

¼ lb. liver (calf's or sheep's preferably), ½ lb. onions, salt, pepper, oil

Slice onions very finely. Cover the bottom of a heavy frying pan (if your pan is lightweight, keep an asbestos mat underneath) with a thin layer of oil. Put in the onions, and cook gently, covered, for 30–40 minutes, with a little salt and pepper. Meanwhile, with a very sharp knife, shave thinnest possible slices off the liver. If it is calf's liver it will only need 2 or 3 minutes cooking with the onions, but if it is sheep or ox liver you will need to add it to the onions after about half an hour and cook for another 15 minutes.

You can serve this just as it is, or with plain boiled rice. It is a particularly warming dish in winter.

BRAISED RED CABBAGE AND FRANKFURTERS (2 *generous helpings*)

1 small red cabbage, 1 large onion, 1 large cooking apple (optional), 2 oz. butter, 1 Tbs. brown sugar, 1 Tbs. vinegar, salt, pepper, 6–8 frankfurters

Remove outside cabbage leaves and slice and chop the cabbage including the core. Peel and roughly chop the onion and cored apple. Put a lump of butter in a heavy pan over gentle heat, add vegetables and spoon them around for a minute till the butter is distributed throughout. Mix vinegar and brown sugar and pour over the cabbage. Cover tightly and cook over very low heat until the cabbage is tender, about 1½ hours. Add salt and pepper to taste. Ten minutes or so before dishing up bury the frankfurters well down among the cabbage, cover, and leave them to heat up.

This dish can be cooked equally well in the oven (gas 3, 325°F., 150°C.) but you will have to leave it for rather longer – 3½ hours would not be excessive. Unlike most vegetable dishes this improves with keeping. Some people like small twists of orange peel cooked with it. I usually serve it with plain boiled potatoes and lots of mustard.

ONION, BACON AND POTATO HOTPOT (*4 helpings*)

If I were restricted to cooking the same three recipes for the rest of my life, this would definitely be on the list. I got it from my mother, who can't remember where she got it from, and friends and acquaintances have been copying it ever since. It is very cheap, makes use of ingredients generally to hand, and tastes – I think – particularly delicious in a homely sort of way.

4 large onions, 4 large potatoes, ¼–½ lb. bacon rashers, 1 pint milk, 2 oz. flour, 2 oz. butter, salt, pepper

First, make some white sauce. Melt the butter, stir in the flour and add the cold milk, stirring occasionally, until the mixture boils and thickens (*see* p. 43). Add salt and pepper, and nutmeg if you like, and leave the sauce simmering gently on an asbestos mat while you prepare the rest of the dish.

Peel and slice onions and potatoes. The onions, which take longer to cook, need to be sliced extra thin. Remove the rind and cut the bacon into smallish strips. Grease a casserole with a lid. Fill it with alternate layers of sliced onions, sliced potatoes and bacon strips, ending with a layer of potato. Pour over the white sauce. Give the casserole a good shake to distribute the sauce throughout. Cover, and bake in fairly hot oven (gas 6, 400°F., 205°C.) for 1 hour. Uncover and bake a further hour at reduced heat (gas 4, 325°F., 150°C.).

The bacon need not be rashers – scraps of cooked bacon left-over from a boiled joint will do just as well. You can use more or less bacon, as convenient. A couple of Tbs. of grated cheese can be added to the white sauce. This is really a winter dish, and goes best with winter vegetables like brussels sprouts and cabbage.

BACON, ONION AND APPLE FRY-UP (*3–4 helpings*)

Scraps from a bacon joint can be excessively salty. The use of apple and onion in this recipe pleasantly counteracts this.

Approximately ½ lb. cooked bacon scraps, trimmed of excess fat, 1 large or 2 medium onions, 2–3 cooking apples, butter or bacon fat for frying, small glass cider (optional)

Peel and roughly chop onions, peel, core and slice apples. Melt fat or butter in frying pan, add onions and fry gently till they begin to soften. Then add sliced apple and continue frying gently for a few minutes. You may need to add a little more butter or fat at this stage. Shake the pan to prevent sticking. When the apple is mushy, add the bacon scraps – diced for appearance's sake – and heat through gently for a few minutes. You may like to add a pinch of brown sugar for extra sweetness. Or, if you like a bit of juice with these dishes, pour in a little cider just before adding the bacon. Serve with plain boiled potatoes.

QUICK-FRIED CHINESE BEEF AND CABBAGE* (*2 helpings*)

The method used here is the same as for Shrimps and Peas (*see* p. 125). The only difference is that the beef, cabbage and onion have to be sliced or shredded beforehand, so it takes a little longer.

¼ lb. slice of lean beef, ½ small white cabbage or 1 green cabbage, 1 onion, 2 cloves garlic, small piece stem ginger, 1–2 Tbs. soya sauce, dash of vinegar, cornflour, oil, Patna rice

First put lots of salted water on to boil for the rice – I allow 6 oz. for two people. Then prepare the beef and vegetables. The meat should be cut with a sharp knife into strips not much larger than a matchstick – slice your piece into thin strips, then turn these over flat and slice them lengthways into even smaller ones. Put them on a small plate. Now shred the cabbage finely, including the stalky part, but discarding ragged outer leaves. If using white cabbage, parboil for a minute or two and drain. Chop the onion finely. Chop garlic and ginger together. Put rice on to boil – timing it for 12 minutes cooking. Heat a little oil in a frying pan. Mix ½ Tbs. cornflour with a little water and soya sauce in a cup.

First gently fry the chopped ginger and garlic, then add chopped onion, then the beef, stirring till it browns lightly all over. Now add the shredded cabbage. Stir for a minute or two, add a spoonful of hot liquid to the cornflour mixture, stir, and then pour this into the frying pan, stirring well to spread it about. Leave the mixture simmering, while you drain, wash and dry off the rice. If the liquid has evaporated too much, add some more hot water and soya sauce. A dash of vinegar can be added too. Serve the rice piled in bowls or soup plates with the beef–cabbage mixture on top and more soya sauce handy for those that like it.

The poorer Chinese families, the peasants, particularly, live almost exclusively on dishes like these where a small amount of meat is padded out, economically, with a lot of vegetables, and the whole is cooked rapidly, both for convenience, and to preserve the natural flavour of the ingredients. Like all good peasant food it achieves an instinctive balance between proteins (meat, fish or poultry), vitamins (vegetables), and carbohydrates (rice). I suggested cabbage here because it is available all the year round, but green beans, green pepper (which must be parboiled), celery or onions would also be suitable. Carrots and cauliflower find their way into dishes in many Chinese restaurants, but their flavour is too overpowering to be successful, I think. You can substitute pork, cut the same way, or slivers of chicken, for the beef. And if you can include some authentically Chinese ingredients – fresh bean sprouts, tinned water chestnut or Chinese radish, the result will be better still.

PORK AND BEANS* (4–6 helpings)

This recipe is a classic of American domestic cookery and the inspiration, I imagine, of the ubiquitous baked beans.

1 lb. haricot beans, ½ lb. streaky pork (salt or otherwise), 1 large onion, dash of Worcestershire Sauce, 2 Tbs. black treacle, 1 dessertspoon brown sugar, 1 dessertspoon powdered mustard, salt, pepper

Soak the haricot beans overnight. Cook them for 1½–2 hours in the water they were soaked in. Strain the beans and keep the water. Cut the streaky pork into chunks, removing any rind. Peel and slice the onion. Heat the bean water and stir into it the treacle, Worcestershire Sauce, mustard, sugar, salt and pepper. Mix up the beans, pork and onion in a casserole, pour over the bean water and add hot water if necessary to come just over the top of the beans. Cover and bake in a moderate oven (gas 4, 350°F., 180°C.) for about an hour, or until the beans are soft. During this time, if the beans seem to be getting too dry, add more hot water.

This is a rich, sweetish dish, and goes best with an uncloying vegetable – spring greens, spinach, braised celery for instance.

CASSEROLED CUTLETS (*2 helpings*)

Buy 2 lamb cutlets – scrag end of neck – per head. You will also need two rashers of bacon, chopped, 1 onion and 1 potato, sliced, and whatever else you have in the vegetable line – a sliced carrot, turnip, a few mushrooms, peas

Put a layer of vegetables on the bottom of a small casserole, then the cutlets, and bacon, then another layer of vegetables. Mix up enough tomato purée and water to cover, add a little salt, pepper, a pinch of sugar and a sprig of thyme or rosemary, or a bayleaf. Pour over the contents of the casserole. Cover. Cook in hot oven (gas 7, 425°F., 220°C.), for half an hour, then reduce heat to gas 3, 325°F., 150°C., and continue cooking for 1–1½ hours.

Serve with rice or mashed potatoes and any other vegetable you fancy.

Alternatively, by using the same cutlets, rather more sliced onion and carrot, 1 sliced turnip, 1 Tbs. pearl barley and a bouillon cube to flavour the liquid instead of tomato concentrate, and cooking in the same way, you will have Irish stew. If possible leave the stew to cool for a few hours, skim off the fat, add a few peas to it and a dash of Worcestershire Sauce and re-heat in a low oven for ½ hour before serving. This should be eaten with boiled potatoes.

FARMHOUSE RABBIT (*4 helpings*)

A very English way of cooking rabbit, particularly suited to the delicate flavour of fresh, wild rabbit, if you can get hold of it. Rabbit is often compared with chicken in point of flavour and texture, but I think it unfair to both, because rabbit, especially wild rabbit, has a flavour all its own, slightly sharp and herb-scented. This recipe steam-bakes the rabbit, which comes out very white and tender with a layer of crunchy stuffing on top.

1 rabbit, 5 large onions, hunk of stale white bread, bacon fat, dripping or butter, 1 Tbs. sage (fresh or dried), pinch of thyme half lemon rind grated, salt and pepper

Ask the butcher to joint the rabbit for you. Leave the pieces of rabbit in salted water while you make the stuffing. For the stuffing, chop onions roughly, cover with water in a pan and bring to the boil. Strain off the water. Soak a thick round of stale bread (3–4 inches) in cold water for a minute and squeeze dry. Tear the bread into small pieces and mix with the par-boiled onions, herbs, grated lemon rind, salt and pepper and a little bacon fat, dripping or butter. Stir the ingredients thoroughly together.

Grease a baking tin. Take the rabbit joints out of the water, shake but do not dry them. Spread the stuffing thickly over all the pieces of rabbit. If your baking tin has a lid, put this on for the first hour of cooking – another baking tin inverted would do. Otherwise, cover with a piece of greased paper or foil, pressing it well down to keep the steam in. Cook at gas 7, 450°F., 232°C. After 1 hour, remove the lid or paper and cook for another hour till the stuffing is crisp and brown on top.

Boiled potatoes and carrots, with a little butter and sugar, are particularly good with this.

RABBIT MARENGO (*4 helpings*)

1 young rabbit cut into serving pieces, 3 Tbs. olive oil, 1 small onion, 1 clove garlic, 1 Tbs. chopped parsley, 1 Tbs. tomato paste, ½ pint water, ¼ lb. mushrooms or mushroom stalks, salt, pepper, a small knob of butter, juice of ½ lemon

Heat olive oil in a large frying pan till it smokes. Fry the rabbit, turning the pieces frequently, till browned all over. Transfer the rabbit to a dish in the oven to keep warm (gas 1, 250°F., 120°C.) while you make the sauce. Put the oil in which the rabbit was cooked into a saucepan and stir in the finely chopped onion and garlic, parsley, tomato paste (tomato concentrate in a tube is best for this), butter and water. Mix well and simmer for a minute or two. Add sliced mushrooms to this sauce and cook till tender, stirring occasionally. Add lemon juice (or 1 Tbs. wine vinegar), salt and pepper to taste, and pour the sauce over the rabbit pieces. Cover the dish and cook for 45 minutes in a moderate oven (gas 4, 350°F., 190°C.).

Serve with plain boiled rice, peas or beans.

Frozen chickens, quartered and cooked as above, are improved by the Marengo Sauce.

BRAISED VEAL (*4–6 helpings*)

Most cuts of veal are formidably expensive, but breast of veal is worth looking out for as it is reasonably priced and less fatty than most breast meat. A little extra time spent trimming the meat into neat chunks, removing as much membrane and fat as possible, improves the appearance of this dish. If you can persuade the butcher to throw in a veal bone or two, they greatly enrich the stock.

2 lb. breast of veal and odd bones, 1 large onion, 2 carrots, 2 celery stalks, 2 Tbs. tomato purée, 1 clove garlic, twist lemon peel, parsley, 1 Tbs. flour, pinch sugar, salt, pepper, 1 oz. butter

Melt the butter in a heavy casserole. Salt, pepper and flour the chunks of veal. Brown them lightly in the butter. Add the bones, cleaned, sliced vegetables, garlic, twist of lemon peel and enough cold water to cover. Bring to the boil, skimming off the froth as it rises to the top. Reduce heat to simmering point, add the tomato purée and sugar and continue simmering gently, covered, for about 1½ hours. Remove the bones and go on cooking uncovered while you prepare the boiled rice which should accompany this dish. Taste the stock to see if it needs more salt and pepper and, just before serving, sprinkle with chopped parsley.

ROAST HAND OF PORK WITH SAGE AND ONION STUFFING
(6–8 helpings)

Pork is the most succulent and one of the cheaper meats for roasting. This particular cut was first suggested to me by my excellent butcher as being the best all-round value from the point of view of price, flavour and general meatiness. Butchers themselves, he tells me, favour a roast hand and they should know. A point to remember when roasting pork is that it should always be over- rather than underdone. Thirty-five to forty minutes per pound in a moderate oven is about right, and a bit longer will do no harm at all. The traditional sage and onion stuffing, sharpened with grated lemon rind, is still the best accompaniment, I think. For greater convenience I suggest cooking it separately from the meat, in a pan on the rack below.

1 hand of pork weighing 3–4 lb., salt

Have the butcher score the rind for you. Rub salt well into the surface of the joint. This encourages crisp crackling. Lay the joint in a roasting pan and put into a pre-heated oven (gas 4, 350°F., 180°C.). Cook for 35–40 minutes per lb., basting with the juices from the pan from time to time. When roast is done transfer to a hot dish and keep it warm while you make the gravy. To do this, pour off the clear fat into a bowl, add a little hot water to the meat juices in the roasting pan, stir over a hotplate on top of the stove, detach all the little particles of meat sticking to the sides and bottom. Add a pinch of salt, pour off into a heated jug and it is ready to serve.

Stuffing: 4 oz. stale white bread, ½ lb. onions, 1 Tbs. fresh or dried sage, grated rind of ½ lemon, 1½–2 oz. butter, salt, pepper

Peel and chop the onions. Put them in a pan of cold water, bring to boil and simmer 4 minutes. Drain well. If you are using fresh sage leaves chop them finely. Mix crumbs, sage, onion and grated lemon rind together thoroughly in a bowl. Soften the butter for a minute or two in the oven. Mix well with the stuffing. Season with salt and pepper. Spread the stuffing in a layer about 1 inch thick in a flat fireproof dish. Cover with a piece of buttered paper and cook on the rack below the roast. After 1 hour or so remove the paper. If the stuffing seems to be getting too dry, spoon a little of the juice from the roast over it.

Vegetables Plus

The following are ways of cooking everyday vegetables to make them good enough to eat on their own.

BUTTERED CARROTS

Small new carrots are best for this, but older ones will serve if well scraped and sliced thinly lengthways, discarding the woody centre.

Parboil carrots by plunging them, whole if new, into boiling salted water for 5 minutes. Drain. Melt a knob of butter in a pan, add a pinch of sugar, a little salt, and some finely chopped garlic and parsley. Cover, and simmer gently till the carrots are tender.

OVEN-COOKED PEAS

Peas today means frozen peas nine times out of ten. Cooked like this they taste something like the real thing. Remember to allow a good hour's cooking time – they can go on a lower rack while your joint or chicken is roasting above.

Put the frozen peas into a shallow casserole with a lid. Add a spoonful of sugar, a sprig of mint (dried in winter), and about 1 oz. of butter cut up small. *No* water. Cover and bake for at least an hour.

BRAISED CELERY

Wash and cut celery sticks discarding soggy or ragged outer ones, into short lengths. Parboil in salted water for 5 minutes. Drain (the water is useful for vegetable soup), and put in a shallow casserole with a little salt, pepper and nutmeg, and plenty of butter. Cover and braise slowly, as for peas, for 1 hour.

GREEN BEANS PROVENÇALE

These should be the stringless French beans, but the same method can be used for ordinary green beans at the start of the season, when they are reasonably small and tender.

If using French beans, top and tail them, if ordinary runner beans, cut off the strings. Put them into boiling salted water and cook till tender, about 8–10 minutes. Drain. Melt a lump of butter in a pan over gentle heat with a clove of garlic. Add the beans and stir till they have absorbed the butter. Meanwhile, pound 2 anchovies till smooth and stir into the beans. Remove garlic before serving.

The anchovies give a subtle but not fishy flavour. Beans cooked like this are good cold but in that case use oil instead of butter and squeeze a little lemon juice over them.

BRUSSELS SPROUTS AND CHESTNUTS

Chestnuts are a nuisance to prepare but they combine very well with sprouts. This is the perfect accompaniment to festive dishes like roast turkey or ham.

Cook the sprouts and chestnuts separately, using about half as many chestnuts as sprouts. Boil the sprouts in salted water till just tender – they should be slightly underdone. Make an incision in the pointed end of the chestnuts and boil for 12 minutes. Peel the chestnuts – shells and inner skins – a few at a time, keeping the rest hot in the water. Melt a lump of butter in a pan and put drained sprouts and chestnuts in together and shake them about till buttery. Salt and pepper them and, if you can, add a spoonful of juices from the roast. Cook together a couple of minutes longer and serve.

CAULIFLOWER ROMAN STYLE

Cauliflower responds to imaginative cooking. This is a delicious recipe, substantial enough for a light meal on its own.

Divide the cauliflower into flowerets. Blanch them in boiling salted water for 3–4 minutes. Drain well. Heat 1 Tbs. oil in a frying pan with 2 cloves of garlic, chopped, and some chopped parsley. Add the cauliflower and let it colour a little. Stir in 2 Tbs. tomato purée, or a few drained peeled tomatoes with a pinch of sugar and salt. Cook for a few minutes, shaking the pan from time to time. Just before serving sprinkle with grated cheese.

BAKED TOMATOES

A delicious way of cooking tomatoes as a vegetable dish. It keeps all their delicate natural flavour. You can use the slightly squashy tomatoes sold for frying, if you cut the bruised bits off. 2–3 tomatoes per person, depending on their size, butter, brown sugar, salt, pepper, breadcrumbs

Cut tomatoes into thick slices and arrange them in a shallow fireproof dish. Sprinkle with salt, pepper and a teaspoon or so of brown sugar. Dab on 1–2 oz. butter cut into tiny pieces. Strew with breadcrumbs. Bake in moderate oven (gas 4, 350°F., 180°C.) for about 20 minutes.

You should use home-made crumbs (*see* p. 114). The kind

sold in packets do nothing for food. These tomatoes go well with fish pies, and you can cook them on a lower grid in the oven at the same time.

FRENCH FRIED ONION RINGS

There is a trick to making these crisp, puffy golden fried onion rings, which is worth learning. Most men will eat almost anything provided you dish up a pile of these onions at the same time.

You need sliced onions, flour, salt and oil or fat to fry them. If you have a deep fryer so much the better.

Sprinkle the sliced onions, which have been very thinly sliced in rings, with salt and leave on a plate for 20 minutes or so, to sweat out their moisture. Then drain, shake off excess salt, dredge with flour (the easiest way to do this is put the flour in a paper bag and shake the onions around inside it) and fry in hot fat or oil.

After 5 minutes – this is the trick – take them out with a perforated slice. Still soft and white. Re-heat the fat till good and hot and put your onions back till they are as crisp and golden as you want them.

N.B. This is also the French method of producing those delicious *frites* (chips) which taste so different from the sluggish white things most chippies produce. The trick is to fry twice, with a pause in between for the fat to heat up again.

STUFFED CABBAGE* (*4–6 helpings*)

There are dozens of recipes for this dish, which is a well-established favourite in almost every country in Europe – except England, where cabbage is not usually given such respectful treatment. The version I use, given here, is quicker to prepare than most, not very elegant perhaps, but tastes just as good.

1 good-sized green cabbage (choose the kind with thick, sturdy leaves), butter, $\frac{1}{2}$ lb. mince or sausage meat, 2 onions, 2 cloves garlic, thyme, parsley, a dash of soya sauce. For the liquid to braise it in, you need $\frac{3}{4}$–1 pint tomato sauce (*see* p. 41), or the same amount of stock, or either of the two mixed with cider

Trim the stalk and the ragged outer leaves off the cabbage. Plunge into boiling water and cook, covered, for 5–6 minutes. Drain.

Prepare the stuffing by melting a little butter in a frying pan and gently frying the chopped onions till they begin to soften. Add the meat, thyme and chopped garlic. When this has browned a little, add a dash of soya sauce. Turn off the heat and stir in a tablespoon or so of chopped parsley.

Now peel back two layers of leaves round your cabbage, taking care not to break them. With a sharp pointed knife cut the centre of the cabbage out, leaving a wall all round and doing your best not to cut through the outer case. This is not all that easy to do – perhaps the best way is to start by removing a small core and hollowing the rest out with a spoon. Pack the stuffing into the cavity. Put a cap on top from the part you cut out, fold the outer leaves back into place and tie with string. Place the cabbage in a deep round casserole, pour on the sauce or stock, packing in any remaining odd bits of cabbage, chopped coarsely, and bake covered for 1–2 hours in a medium oven. If you are in a hurry, cook it at gas 6, 400°F., 205°C. for 1 hour, and a few degrees lower if you want to leave it for a couple of hours. Spoon a little of the liquid over it from time to time.

All you need with this is boiled rice.

BAKED, STUFFED VEGETABLE MARROW* (*4 or more helpings*)

Large vegetable marrows are very cheap in season and make a handy receptacle for a highly seasoned mince stuffing, the bland flavour of the marrow providing just enough contrast.

It is a less solid and indigestible dish than stuffed green peppers or aubergines, and I think rather nicer.

1 medium-sized marrow (about 1 foot long), ½ lb. minced beef or lamb, 2 or 3 rashers of bacon, 2 onions, garlic, thyme or marjoram or fennel, salt, pepper, 4 oz. cooked rice, 1 tin peeled tomatoes or tomato purée

Heat a large pan of water and plunge the marrow in when boiling and cook for 3 minutes. Remove. Slice off the top of the marrow, longitudinally, about one third from the top so you have one deeper marrow receptacle and one shallow lid. Scoop out the seeds and membrane, and a little pulp if the space looks too shallow.

Melt a little butter in a frying pan. Fry bacon cut into small squares and chopped onions and garlic. Add the mince and fry gently till lightly browned. Moisten with juice from peeled tomatoes or a little diluted tomato purée. Add herbs, season well with salt and pepper. Stir in cooked rice. If the mixture seems very dry, add more tomato liquid. (A few raisins, sultanas or currants can be added to this stuffing.) Fill the scooped-out marrow with the mixture, clap on the lid, secure with string or a couple of skewers. Boil up tinned tomatoes with a little salt, sugar and pepper till they can be mashed to a pulp. Dilute with water if it is too thick. Pour this round the marrow, in a baking tin. Bake in a moderate oven for 1 hour, or until the marrow is tender, basting from time to time with the tomato sauce.

Serve with plain boiled rice, and the juice from the pan.

STOVIES* (2 helpings)

¾ lb. potatoes, 3–4 onions, dripping

Melt enough dripping (lard, or lard-and-butter can be used instead but the traditional Scots recipe calls for real meat dripping from a roast) in a heavy, lidded saucepan or casserole to form a $\frac{1}{4}$ inch layer over the bottom. Put in a thick layer of chopped onions and fry slowly, with the lid on, till the onions are almost soft. Then add a layer of potatoes, peeled and sliced, cover and leave to steam fry. When the potatoes are soft take a wooden spoon and turn the mixture over roughly. Salt, pepper and eat.

ONION AND POTATO PURÉE (*2 helpings*)

3 large potatoes, 4 large onions, butter, milk, 2 egg yolks (optional), salt, pepper, nutmeg

For this dish you need roughly equal weights of onions and potatoes. Peel and boil them in salted water. It is probably better to do this in separate saucepans because the onions tend to take longer than the potatoes. They should be very soft. When both vegetables are cooked, drain thoroughly, squeezing as much moisture out of the onions as possible. Both vegetables should now be pushed through a sieve, but if this is too laborious you can achieve similar results by mashing the potatoes with a spoon and chopping the onions to a mush which will go through a sieve quite easily. Stir onions and potato together and add small bits of butter and a little hot milk, whipping it up with a wooden spoon, till you have a light thick purée. Just before serving stir in the egg yolk and season well with salt, pepper and a dash of grated nutmeg.

This makes a pleasant change from straightforward mashed potatoes. It is good with sausages, poached eggs and lamb chops.

N.B. It *is* more trouble to heat the milk before adding it to the purée but it makes it much lighter. The same goes for mashed potatoes.

CORN CHOWDER (*3–4 helpings*)

A poor relation of the celebrated New England chowders, this is a mild but not insipid dish somewhere between a soup and a stew in consistency. Ideal fare for hangovers, or whenever one feels a bit delicate. It can be eaten as a filling first course, or as a meal on its own with a slice of fresh bread.

2–3 bacon rashers, 3 medium-sized potatoes, 1 7-oz. tin sweet corn niblets, 1 pint milk, 1 oz. butter, salt, pepper

Peel and roughly dice potatoes. Cut bacon into small strips. Melt butter in heavy saucepan or cast-iron casserole, add bacon and frizzle for a minute or two. Add diced potato and stir for a couple of minutes. Pour in milk and leave to simmer over low heat till the potatoes are tender. Now add corn niblets and liquid from tin, stir, season with salt and pepper to taste and leave to simmer a few minutes longer. Serve in soup plates.

BOILED POTATO DUMPLINGS*

An elegant way of using up leftover mash. To roughly 1 lb. mashed potatoes you will need 2 eggs, separated, a little chopped parsley, or a pinch of any other fresh herbs available, 1 heaped Tbs. fresh *white* breadcrumbs and a little butter.

Beat up the mashed potatoes and when malleable beat in the egg yolks, parsley or herbs and breadcrumbs. Add more salt and pepper if the mash is insipid, and a trace of grated nutmeg if you like it. Then fold in the stiffly beaten egg whites lightly but thoroughly. Drop a spoonful at a time into boiling salted water, cover and simmer till the dumplings rise to the top, which means they are cooked (about 10 minutes). Remove with a perforated spoon and drain.

You can serve these simply with melted butter, or in recognition of their kinship with Gnocchi, with a powdering of grated Parmesan over them, browned lightly under the grill.

The Pauper's Cookbook

CELERY, BEETROOT AND ONION SALAD (4 helpings)

If you find beetroot cloying on its own, try this excellent winter salad, where the sweetness of the beet is offset by the crisp texture of celery and pungent taste of onion.

2 medium-sized cooked beetroots, 4 or 5 celery stalks, 1 mild onion, dressing

Peel the beets and cut into dice. Scrub the celery well and cut crossways into thin strips. Slice the onion finely and separate the rings. Combine all the ingredients. Add dressing to taste and if possible leave for a few hours before eating.

An ordinary vinaigrette dressing is quite adequate for this but if you want to glorify the salad the following vinaigrette-plus will do the trick.

Mix together 1 Tbs. vinegar, 3 Tbs. oil, salt, pepper, 1 tsp. made English or French mustard, 1 tsp. brown sugar, the sieved yolks of 2 hard-boiled eggs, a squeeze of lemon juice, salt, pepper. Beat this lot up together till it is a smooth emulsion and stir it into your salad – you may not need it all, so use your discretion. Just before serving stir in a couple of spoonfuls of cream.

COLESLAW* (4 helpings)

Coleslaw is a very useful standby in winter, when the usual salad materials are expensive. Shredded raw cabbage – the hard, white type is the best – provides the bulk of the salad, and you can vary the other ingredients according to what you have in the way of vegetables. It is a good idea to make it an hour or so ahead, mix the dressing in and leave it standing. If you are interested in the health aspect, a salad like this is packed with Vitamins, especially Vitamin C.

You will need a quarter to a half of a cabbage, depending on the size, 1 or 2 carrots, a large sweet apple, a couple of sticks of celery and a little onion – if you like the taste of raw onion

Shred the cabbage as finely as possible with a sharp knife and leave it to crisp in a bowl of cold water while you prepare the rest of the vegetables. Peel and grate the carrots, peel core and chop the apple into dice, wash the celery and cut into thin strips, grate or slice the onion finely. Dry the cabbage carefully and mix all the vegetables together. Dress with a vinaigrette dressing to which you have added a little lemon juice, mustard and brown sugar.

I find a sprinkling of fresh thyme – grown in a flowerpot on the windowsill – helps this salad. Dried thyme can be substituted. And you can throw in chopped walnuts, sultanas, grated cheese, raw shredded Brussels sprouts, shredded celeriac, and so on as the fancy takes you.

TOMATO SALAD

One of the simplest and nicest of all salads, to indulge in freely when tomatoes are cheap and ripe. Eat it on its own, as the French do, as an hors d'œuvre, or with cold dishes like rice salad, or fish and aioli.

The tomatoes should be firm and ripe. Pour boiling water over them for a minute or two, pour off, rinse under cold water and you will find the skins come off easily. Slice the tomatoes crosswise into a dish. If possible sugar them lightly and leave overnight, which develops the flavour remarkably. Then season with salt and pepper and an oily vinaigrette dressing and sprinkle with chopped chives and fresh herbs, if you want a delicate flavour, or spring onions cut into tiny rings. For a more robust salad, mix the tomatoes with thinly sliced mild onions in whatever proportions you fancy.

CUSTARD SAUCE

The French call this Crème Anglaise. The English, prosaic to the last, usually refer to it as boiled custard. Properly made, it tastes as different from hectic yellow packet custards as Stilton from processed cheese. The French think highly of its digestive properties and often eat it on its own, like a sweet soup.

The proportions are 4 egg yolks to 1 pint milk and 1 Tbs. sugar. You can flavour it with 1 tsp. vanilla essence, or better still with a split vanilla pod

Beat up yolks with a fork. Heat milk slowly with the sugar and split vanilla pod, to boiling point. Remove from heat, take out the pod (if a few black specks remain, don't worry, these are harmless, besides being pleasantly flavoured), and pour the milk on to the yolks. Stir, return to pan and heat over simmering water (double-boiler method) till the mixture thickens and coats the back of your wooden spoon. Leave to cool.

N.B. It is only fair to mention that there is a hazard in making this type of custard, which is that you may cook it too long or too fiercely, so the eggs curdle. If you don't trust your judgement you can prevent this by adding 1 scant Tbs. cornflour, diluted in a little cold milk, to your mixture. The custard needs to be cooked a little longer till the cornflour taste has gone. Chefs might raise their eyebrows, but this need hardly affect you.

RICE PUDDING (*4 helpings*)

It is surprising how few rice puddings taste the way they should, neither stodgy nor gritty, but tender, creamy and mellow. There is no mystery to making a successful rice pudding – it depends on using the right proportions of rice to milk, and long slow cooking.

The proportions (remember these because they are the same

for all milk and cereal puddings) are 2 Tbs. pudding rice to
1 pint milk. You also need 2–3 Tbs. sugar, depending how
sweet you like it, a little vanilla essence or a vanilla pod cooked
with the pudding, and a few dabs of butter

Wash the rice. Butter a shallow oven dish lightly. Pour in the
milk, add the rice and sugar and stir to distribute them evenly.
Add a little vanilla essence or a vanilla pod. Dot a few little
pieces of butter on top and put into a slow oven (gas 3, 325°F.,
150°C.). After ½ hour or so, when a skin has formed on top, stir
the skin into the pudding. Repeat this about an hour later. The
pudding will be cooked in 2½ hours. If you are cooking something else in the oven at the same time put the pudding on a
lower shelf, the bottom shelf if the oven is hot.

An alternative way of cooking rice is to use the top of a
double boiler, cooking it for 3–4 hours, over barely simmering
water, till all the milk is absorbed. Use the same ingredients and
proportions as for the first method. In the Middle East rice
cooked like this is mixed with thick, or whipped cream, and
served very cold with a powdering of cinnamon.

SPICED APPLE PURÉE (*4 helpings*)

Most apple purées are plain stewed apples given a hopeful and
vigorous stir with a wooden spoon. The result is a watery mush.
It takes a minute longer to convert this into the proper velvet-
smooth consistency, but this minute – as with so many simple
recipes – is crucial.

2 lb. cooking apples, sugar to taste, 4 cloves, cinnamon, 1 oz.
butter

Peel, core and slice the apples. Heat gently with the cloves
and a pinch of cinnamon in enough water just to cover. When
the apples are soft, add sugar to taste. Now put them through a
fine sieve, removing the cloves. The sieving is vital because it

removes the little fibres and gives a smooth purée – use a hair or plastic sieve if possible. Now stir in the butter. Leave to cool.

Serve with cream or custard sauce, made the proper way with eggs and milk and a little vanilla (*see* p. 76).

POLISH APPLE CHARLOTTE

2 lb. cooking apples, sugar, lemon rind, butter, 4 crushed macaroons, 2 Tbs. marmalade

Core, peel and stew the apples in a little water with sugar to sweeten, and a little shaving of lemon peel to flavour them. When they are cooked, sieve them, stir in a knob of butter and cover with a crust of crushed macaroons, mixed with enough marmalade to bind them together. Bake 20 minutes in a moderate oven (gas 4, 350°F., 180°C.).

Serve with cream.

RASPBERRY CRUMBLE (*4 helpings*)

Tinned raspberries are good value, with a fresher flavour than most tinned fruit, and they make a nice variation on the classic apple crumble.

1 lb. tinned raspberries, 6 oz. plain flour, 1 tsp. baking powder, 3 oz. butter, 4 oz. vanilla sugar or soft brown sugar plus a tiny pinch ground ginger

Drain the raspberries of most of their juice. Put them in a shallow fireproof dish.

Make the crumble by sifting the flour, ginger and baking powder together into a bowl. Cut the butter into small pieces, then cut these into the flour with a knife until as well mixed as possible. Add the sugar and rub this lightly into the flour and butter with the fingertips, till the mixture forms crumbs. Spread the crumbs lightly in a smooth layer over the raspberries, but don't press them down.

Bake in a fairly hot oven (gas 6, 400°F., 205°C.) for 30–40 minutes, until the crumble feels slightly crisp on top.

Serve with cream, or with the remainder of the raspberry syrup, heated up with a little water and 1 tsp. or so of cornflour till it looks thick and clear.

PEACH UPSIDE-DOWN PUDDING (4–6 *helpings*)

1 large tin peach slices, 3 oz. butter, 6 oz. brown sugar

Batter: 4 oz. sifted plain flour, 1½ tsp. baking powder, 6 oz. sugar, pinch salt, 2 eggs, 6 Tbs. hot water, 1 tsp. vanilla essence

Drain the peach slices. Melt butter and brown sugar over moderate heat in cake pan or baking tin. Remove from heat and arrange peach slices in rows on top of the butter/sugar mixture in the bottom of the pan.

Sift flour, baking powder and salt together. Beat the egg yolks in a large bowl, till pale yellow and fluffy. Add sugar gradually, beating well after each addition. Then add hot water, a little at a time, still beating, and finally the flour, by degrees. Beat all well, till thoroughly mixed. Then fold in stiffly beaten egg whites and pour the batter over the peaches. Bake in hottish oven (gas 6, 400°F., 205°C.) for 40 minutes. Let the pudding stand for 5 minutes, then invert it on to a large plate but leave the tin over it for 10–15 minutes longer so that the caramel can drip over the cake.

APRICOT FOOL (4 *helpings*)

Apricots are quite a reasonable price towards the end of the summer, and they make excellent fool.

1 lb. apricots, 3–4 Tbs. sugar, ⅓–½ pint whipped cream

Cut the apricots in half and take out the stones. Crack 4 or 5 of the stones with a hammer and extract the kernels. The kernels add an extra something to the flavour so this little effort is worth making. Put the apricot halves, kernels and 3 or 4 Tbs. sugar into a fireproof dish, with enough water to cover, and bake in the oven (gas 4, 350°F., 180°C.), till the apricots are soft. Rub them through a sieve. Stir in whipped cream. If you can't run to ½ pint of cream mix a smaller quantity with the beaten white of one egg. Taste to see if the fool is sweet enough to set aside to cool.

BREAD AND BUTTER PUDDING (*4–6 helpings*)

Like most simple dishes, bread-and-butter pudding needs to be made with care. The slices of bread should be really thin, with the crusts removed – but don't give in to the temptation to use packed sliced bread unless you want the pudding to taste like wet flannel.

6 thin slices buttered stale white bread, a handful of raisins or sultanas, 2 eggs and 1 yolk, ¾ pint milk, ½ tsp. vanilla essence, sugar

Cut the bread-and-butter into quarters or triangles. Arrange them in layers in a fireproof dish, with a sprinkling of raisins or sultanas and sugar on each layer. Beat up the 2 eggs and 1 yolk in a bowl and mix with the heated milk flavoured with ½ tsp. vanilla essence. Pour this over the bread and butter. Some people believe in letting the pudding stand for ½ an hour or so before baking. Otherwise sprinkle sugar over the top, dot with a little more butter and bake for 45 minutes to 1 hour in a slow oven (gas 3, 325°F., 150°C.).

Equally good hot or cold, served plain or with cream.

LEMON MERINGUE PIE (*6–8 helpings*)

This is a particularly foolproof version of an American classic. It makes a large pie – you will need a pre-baked 9 inch short crust shell. If this seems too much use half the quantities in a 7 inch shell, but as the pie tastes equally good hot or cold there is usually no trouble with leftovers.

1 pre-baked 9 inch short crust shell (*see* p. 100), 4 egg yolks, 6 oz. sugar, rind and juice of 2 lemons

Meringue: 4 oz. sugar, 4 egg whites

To make the pie filling, beat egg yolks vigorously with sugar, adding the strained juice and grated rind of the lemons. Cook in the top of a double boiler over barely simmering water till thick. Beat the egg whites till stiff and dry with the remaining sugar. Take about half the egg whites and fold into the lemon custard mixture. Pour into the pie shell. Cover with the rest of the egg white, spooning it on lightly so that it looks peaked on top. Brown in moderate oven (gas 4, 350°F., 180°C.) for 15–20 minutes.

GOOSEBERRY SNOW (*4 helpings*)

2 pints gooseberries, 2 Tbs. sugar, just under ¼ pint water, 2 eggs, 1 oz. butter, 1½ Tbs. caster sugar

Stew the gooseberries till soft with water and 4 oz. sugar. Put through a fine sieve, add the butter while warm and mix well. Separate the eggs, beat up the yolks and stir them into the purée when it has cooled slightly. Pour into a pie dish and cook in a moderate oven (gas 4, 350°F., 180°C.) for about 20 minutes, or until the mixture has set.

Remove from oven and, while it is cooling, whisk the egg whites up stiffly, adding the caster sugar little by little. When the meringue mixture is glossy, spread it over the gooseberry custard and bake in a low oven (gas 2, 275°F., 140°C.) until the meringue is set (about 20 minutes).

An ideal pudding to serve when there are children around, with cream.

GOOSEBERRY COMPOTE (*6–8 helpings*)

A compote is a more elegant version of ordinary stewed fruit, the difference being that the fruit is simmered till tender in a thin syrup, rather than stewed in sugared water. This keeps the fruit from disintegrating, and produces a dish with a more concentrated flavour.

1 quart green gooseberries, $\frac{1}{2}$ lb. sugar, 1 pint water, 1 Tbs. apricot jam or redcurrant jelly (optional)

Top and tail the gooseberries and scald in boiling water for 2 minutes. Drain.

In another pan make a syrup of the sugar and water, adding the sugar to the cold water and stirring frequently till it dissolves. Boil the syrup for 10 minutes. Add the jam or jelly. Put the gooseberries into the syrup and simmer gently till tender. Serve cold with thin cream.

RHUBARB PIE★ (*4–6 helpings*)

Rhubarb, as well as being good for you, is still unusually good value. Like most tart fruit, it makes excellent pies. In this recipe the pastry goes underneath, but you could equally well reverse the procedure and have the pastry on top as a cover.

$1\frac{1}{2}$ lb. rhubarb, 1 lemon, 6 oz. brown sugar, 1 Tbs. cornflour, cinnamon, short crust pastry shell (9 inch size)

Partly pre-cook the pastry shell (*see* p. 101, for short crust recipe) for 10–15 minutes (gas 7, 425°F., 220°C.). Wipe but do not peel the rhubarb and cut it into short chunks. Mix the sugar, cornflour, cinnamon, grated rind and juice of the lemon together. Sprinkle half this mixture on the bottom of the shell, lay the cut rhubarb on top and cover with the remaining sugar. If you have any pastry left over make a lattice of little strips on top of the pie, sticking them down round the sides by moistening with a little milk. Bake in a pre-heated oven (gas 6, 400°F., 200°C.) for ¾–1 hour, or until the rhubarb seems tender.

Serve with plain cream.

SHIRLEY'S TIPSY PRUNES

1 lb. prunes, red or white wine

A splendidly simple way to raise prunes to the gourmet class. Half fill a jar with ordinary dried (not soaked) prunes, add wine (leftovers will do) to fill the jar (the prunes expand), cover and leave. Serve as a pudding with a little thin cream or as a relish with plain meat dishes.

Padding

This chapter deals specifically with the art or science of stretching small quantities of food (and money) a bit further. Leftovers are part of the story, but the emphasis here is not so much on what bits and pieces you have to work with as on various ways of expanding them into a solid meal. This is where the idea of padding comes in. Rice and pasta are two examples of padding which need little introduction from me. But there are other less familiar ones – batters, pastry, suet crust, pulses, semolina, soufflé bases – which paupers in particular ought to know about. The reason being, of course, that they are dazzlingly cheap and versatile. A short crust pastry-flan case, for instance. This costs next to nothing to make. Onions, butter, flour and a little cream or top of the milk turn it into a savoury meal for two, or first course for four. Alternatively, a few eggs, 2 lemons and some sugar make it into an impressive Lemon Meringue pie. So, for an outlay of around 25p, you can convert ingredients which would be nothing much on their own into good solid food. Similarly, a trifling outlay on batter makes $\frac{1}{2}$ lb. of chipolatas into a meal for three or four people. A lot of suet crust and a little jam gives you a roly–poly pudding to silence a party of hungry schoolboys. 1 lb. of haricot beans, some belly of pork and a few other odds and ends add up to a hearty dish of Pork and Beans (*see* p. 61), which will feed six comfortably.

No Victorian housewife would have needed reminding of these basic principles of economical cookery. But, with the current craze for high-protein, low-calorie diets, I think many of these padding foods have fallen into disrepute, as being fattening, indigestible and somehow unwholesome. And yet about a quarter of the nation's grocery bills goes on biscuits, and the same people who quail at the sight of a suet pudding will cheerfully consume mountains of crisps, cereals and chocolate bars. The point to remember, I think, is that a normal diet should strike a balance between starch, protein and vitamin foods. The padding foods in this chapter are high in carbo-hydrates, but this only becomes a bad thing, dietetically speaking, if you eat nothing else. A thick lentil soup, followed by steak and kidney pudding and mashed potatoes and a fruit pie, would be too much. Solid dishes need to be balanced by salads, green vegetables, light fruit puddings, thin soups.

Another point I would like to make about the padding foods mentioned in this chapter is that they are not tediously slow and complicated, or difficult, to make. A lot of people are put off attempting pastry, for instance, by the mystique which has grown up round the subject – all that talk about 'light hands', correct temperatures, proportions – which is a pity because pastry-making is a simple process and only requires a few trial runs to be reasonably foolproof. (Short crust and suet crust, that is. I have deliberately excluded the more elaborate varieties like puff and flaky pastry.) Once you are familiar with the procedure you will find it takes about 5 minutes to make pastry, or batters, a couple of minutes with a rolling pin to produce home-made breadcrumbs, 10 minutes in all to produce a soufflé.

Rice

It is astonishing how much disagreement reigns over the best way of boiling rice. This may be because it has only recently been grown in Europe, and a certain mystery still clings to its preparation. Having tried some of the more complicated methods, I am pleased to say that the easiest and quickest also gives the best results.

The best rice for boiling is the long-grain or Patna variety. Round-grain, or Carolina, rice, is suitable for puddings and for risottos where the grains need to be highly absorbent. I generally use rather more rice than specified, just under $\frac{1}{2}$ lb. for two people. Leftovers can be used up as salads, or combined with other ingredients as stuffings.

Heat a large pan of salted water. When boiling, tip in the rice. Boil fast for 12 minutes. Drain in a colander under the hot water tap for a minute to wash off any glutinous starch. To dry off and separate the grains you can either return the rice to the pan and leave it covered over a very low flame for 5–10 minutes, stirring once or twice with a fork to loosen the grains, *or* (which is marginally easier) pour it into a shallow oven dish and put it in a low oven for 10 minutes or so.

RICE SALAD

Cold rice can be mixed with a great variety of bits and pieces and turned into successful salads. Any of the following suggestions can be used in varying combinations, according to what is available: tinned or fresh crab, shrimps, cooked mussels, chopped cooked chicken, ham, garlic sausage, hard-boiled egg, diced cucumber, tomatoes (peeled), raw onion, cooked peas, spring onions, raw mushrooms, cubes of green pepper, diced green beans, beetroot, raisins, sultanas, capers, chopped raw apple, grated carrot, cubes of mild cheese. You will probably be able to think of many more. The main thing is to try and balance the textures and flavours pleasantly – something crisp, something soft, something sharp, something sweet, etc. And dice or chop the ingredients quite small. Rice with large lumps of stuff buried in it looks sloppy and faintly sinister.

When you have combined your chosen ingredients with the rice, season it well with salt and pepper or paprika, moisten liberally with a mild vinaigrette – more oily than vinegary – or thin mayonnaise. And, if possible, sprinkle some chopped fresh herbs or parsley over the dish.

HOT SAVOURY RICE

There are two ways of preparing dishes of savoury rice. The easiest, and I think safest for non-Italians, is to boil the rice and cook up the other ingredients separately, giving them a few minutes together in the pan or oven to merge the flavours just at the end. The other way, more properly the risotto or paella method, is to cook all the ingredients together, first frying the rice, and then adding boiling liquid (stock, water, wine or a mixture of the three) gradually, together with scraps of meat, fish, chicken, vegetables or whatever, until the rice is tender. The second method does produce a richer dish, with a moist, creamy texture, when correctly cooked. But it requires more judgement and concentration on the part of the cook if it is not to turn into an unappetizing sludge, or worse still, a mass of gritty undercooked rice. You do also need a really good heavy cast-iron or earthenware dish to cook it in.

My advice is, practise making risottos or paellas in small quantities, for private consumption, but avoid the common mistake of serving them up as a cheap omnibus meal for dinner guests until you are confident of getting the right results. In the meantime, the other method, or the method used in making Suleiman's Pilaff, a compromise between the two, will save a lot of nervous strain.

CHICKEN LIVER PILAFF (*4 helpings*)

A hot, savoury rice dish made by the first method described above. Chicken livers can often be bought very cheaply at chicken barbecues, as well as at some fishmongers and butchers. When buying livers in quantities like this, though, make sure you go through them carefully before cooking, removing any greenish discoloured parts. These stains are caused by perforated gall bladders and have a very bitter taste.

1 lb. Patna rice, ¼ lb. mushrooms, 1 large onion, 4 rashers bacon, 6 oz. chicken livers, 2 oz. butter, 2 cubes chicken bouillon, 1 oz. almonds, salt, pepper, paprika

Dissolve the bouillon cubes in 1 quart boiling water. Add rice, but no salt as the bouillon is salty, and time to cook for 12 minutes.

Meanwhile melt half the butter in a frying pan and cook the bacon, de-rinded and cut into small squares, over moderate heat till the fat begins to run. Now add roughly chopped onion and continue frying gently till golden. At this point add the chicken livers, cut into small pieces. When these are cooked through, which should take only 2–3 minutes, add the sliced mushrooms. Fry gently, stirring from time to time, till the mushrooms are tender. Taste and add salt and pepper as needed.

The rice should now be cooked. Drain in a sieve or colander but do not rinse under hot tap as this would wash off the chicken flavour. Turn into an oven dish. Mix in the liver mixture lightly but thoroughly with a fork. Dot with the rest of the butter and leave in a low oven (gas 3, 325°F., 150°C.) for 20 minutes. While the pilaff is heating through, melt some butter in a small pan and fry the almonds till crisp and golden.

Sprinkle them over the pilaff, together with a little paprika, just before serving.

A crisp green salad goes well with this dish.

SULEIMAN'S PILAFF (*4–6 helpings*)

An excellent way of using up small bits and pieces of cooked lamb left over from a joint.

1 lb. Patna rice, olive oil or dripping, 4–6 oz. cooked lamb cut into smallish cubes, 2–3 onions, 2 cloves garlic, 4 fresh or 1 small tin peeled tomatoes, 1 Tbs. currants and sultanas, salt, pepper, a pinch of thyme or rosemary

The rice is fried before boiling to make it richer. In a heavy pan melt a good lump of dripping, or 3 Tbs. olive oil, and fry the rice gently, stirring till it begins to look transparent. Now pour 2 quarts boiling water over the rice and boil fast, uncovered, for about 12 minutes or until the rice is tender. Strain and return to the pan, and leave it covered over a tiny flame.

In the meantime, fry up the other ingredients in oil or dripping, starting with the chopped onions and garlic and adding chopped tomatoes, dried fruit and herbs, when these are golden. Season generously and simmer gently till the ragoût is thick and tasty. Add the diced meat, trimmed of most of the fat, towards the end – too much cooking is liable to toughen it.

Stir the meat mixture into the rice, adding more dripping if you think it needs it. Cook over gentle heat for a few minutes longer and serve.

In the Middle East a savoury pilaff would be served with yoghourt or sour cream stirred into it. If that idea does not appeal to you, try serving a salad of thinly sliced cucumber dressed with a little yoghourt or sour cream and a few finely chopped mint leaves, along with the pilaff. Alternatively the Turkish Salad (*see* p. 171), made with oranges and onions, would be a refreshing combination.

RISOTTO WITH MUSSELS* (*2 helpings*)

1 quart mussels, 6 oz. Carolina rice, 1 onion, 2 cloves garlic, 1 Tbs. grated Parmesan, 1½ pints mussel stock, salt, pepper, nutmeg

To prepare the mussels, rinse them well in cold running water. Scrape the shells and pull off the stringy beards – I use a pair of pliers. Discard any mussels which are not tightly closed. Rinse again in running water. Heat 1½ pints water to boiling point in a large pan and tip in the mussels when it is bubbling. As soon as they have all opened, strain off the cooking water into a large bowl – you will be using it to make the risotto – and leave the mussels in the pan till they are cool enough to handle, when they should be removed from their shells. Keep them warm at the side of the stove till the time comes to add them to the risotto.

To make the risotto first set the mussel cooking water to simmer in a pan. In another heavy pan melt 1 Tbs. butter or oil, or a mixture of the two. Add finely chopped onion and garlic and cook over moderate heat till pale golden. Add the rice, stirring till it has absorbed the oil or fat, which will take approximately 1 minute. Now add a cupful of simmering mussel stock, shaking the pan till the rice has absorbed it, add another cupful, and so on till most of the hot liquid has been absorbed and the rice is swollen and beginning to feel tender. You will need to stir continuously with a wooden spoon (or better still, a wooden fork) at this stage to prevent the rice sticking. If the mussel liquor seems to be giving out before the rice is done, use a little boiling water instead. Towards the end of the cooking time, somewhere between 20 and 30 minutes depending on the absorbency of the rice, stir in the mussels and add salt, pepper and a dusting of grated nutmeg to taste. Just before serving, stir in the grated cheese and another lump of butter. The knack with risotto – which only comes with practice – is to tell just when the rice is perfectly cooked, neither gritty nor sticky.

Mussels are only one of many possible additions to a basic white risotto. Shreds of cooked ham, chicken, shrimps, are all suitable, as are cooked mushrooms, or even just grated Parmesan and nutmeg.

Barley

Barley is commonly used in small quantities to provide a nutty taste and pleasant texture in soups and stews. For curiosity's sake, though, I have included a recipe for Kasha, in which barley is used where most people would expect rice, with a pleasantly different result.

BARLEY KAIL SOUP* (4–6 helpings)

An old Scots cottage recipe, and highly economical.

2 oz. pearl barley, 1 quart basic stock or water plus a mutton bone and a few scraps of meat, 1 lb. kale, 3 leeks, salt, pepper

Put the barley and stock, or water plus bone and scraps (the bone from a lamb joint would do very well) to simmer for about ¾ hour, or until the barley is tender, skimming off any scum which rises to the surface. Add the kale, washed and cut into thin shreds, with the coarsest stalks removed, also the washed and sliced leeks. Simmer till the vegetables are tender, adding salt and pepper as necessary. Before serving remove the bone and any unsightly scraps of meat.

MUSHROOM KASHA (3–4 helpings)

Kasha is a traditional dish in Russia and Poland. It can be made with buckwheat groats or pearl barley. This version uses barley.

It is a pleasant-looking and tasting dish, with an earthy, nutty flavour, a little reminiscent of wild rice. I find it goes very well with sausages, gammon and braised pigeon. The original recipe uses dried mushrooms, which have a pungent flavour and smell of their own, but I have substituted the ordinary cultivated variety with satisfactory results. The only difference in preparation is that the dried kind need preliminary soaking in warm water.

½ lb. pearl barley, 1 oz. dried or ¼ lb. cultivated mushrooms, 1–2 oz. butter, salt and pepper to taste, 2 Tbs. grated cheese, 1 egg

First beat up the egg and stir it into the barley, so that the grains are well coated, and leave to dry. Soak the mushrooms (if you are using dried mushrooms) in 1 pint warm salted water. Then simmer them, covered, in the same water for ¼ hour or until tender. With cultivated mushrooms, wipe and slice them, then simmer in 1 pint salted water, covered, for ¼ hour. In both cases pour off the mushroom liquor into a bowl, put the mushrooms aside, and return the cooking liquor to the pan. Put a lump of butter into the pan and simmer till melted. Then add the barley, cover, and simmer very slowly for 10 minutes, stirring from time to time. Now transfer the contents of the pan to a small, heavy casserole with a lid. Cast-iron pots were traditionally used for cooking Kasha, but earthenware makes a good substitute. Mix in the mushrooms, cut into small strips, a pinch of salt and a sprinkling of pepper. Put on the lid and bake in a moderate oven (gas 4, 350°F., 180°C.) for 1 hour. Before serving, stir in another lump of butter and the grated cheese.

Oats

It is quite a good idea to have a packet of oats around, even if you do not eat porridge. They are useful for coating herring and mackerel before frying, as the Scots do. A spoonful or two can can be used to thicken soups and stews.

PORRIDGE

Porridge oats – not the instant type – are greatly improved by steeping overnight in milk before cooking. This brings out all their flavour and gives a creamy texture. The proportions per person are roughly 1 oz. oats to 6 fl. oz. milk, plus a pinch of salt. Mix and leave overnight. To cook, bring milk and oats slowly to simmering point and cook gently for 5–8 minutes, or until the porridge thickens. Check that you have added enough salt.

The Scots name for this used to be Crowdie-Mowdie. They also used to steam the oats for 2 hours, but I think that is a refinement which can be disregarded.

SCOTS FRIED HERRING (*2 helpings*)

Herrings are very good rolled in oats, and fried. Allow 1 large or 2 small herrings per head. They can be cooked whole, or split, boned and flattened.

Allow 1 oz. oats and 1 oz. dripping or butter for every 2 herring. Wipe the fish carefully. Salt and pepper them. Sprinkle the oats on a sheet of kitchen paper and toss the fish in them till well coated. Melt the dripping or butter (a dribble of oil will help prevent it burning) in a frying pan and when smoking hot put in the herring and fry till brown on both sides. Whole herring will take 10 minutes, split herring 5. Serve with a wedge of lemon and boiled potatoes.

Pasta

There are, as you doubtless know, dozens of different types of pasta. These vary as to shape, ingredients and the uses to which they are put. Cheapest and most useful for most purposes, I find, are the long packets of spaghetti and macaroni. Egg noodles are good for dishes like Chinese Spiced Beef (*see* p. 179) but more expensive. Decorative shell-shaped pastas are best for using cold, as salads, or in soups.

The cooking time varies from one variety to another, and is usually clearly stated on the packet. Quite often I find the times given are over-generous, and so I start tasting the pasta a good 5 minutes earlier – it should be slightly resistant when you bite it, not soft right through. It should always be put into lots of boiling salted water, in a big pan. A little oil added at the same time will prevent the water boiling over. When it is done, pour into a colander, run hot water through very rapidly to wash off any sticky starch, and return to the pan over a very low heat, with a lump of butter or spoonful of oil, salt and black pepper. Toss it about till it is shining with the fat. It is usually served with a sauce of some kind, or as an accompaniment to a main dish, but it tastes good just as it is, with lots of grated cheese and more butter. A little garlic, chopped almost to a paste with whatever fresh herbs are available, makes an appetizing instant sauce.

To prevent leftover pasta going hard and dry, leave it covered with cold water, and drain before using.

SAVOURY BACON AND NOODLE PIE* (*4 helpings*)

This recipe specifies bacon rashers but roughly similar quantities of leftover ham or gammon would do just as well. A few chopped mushrooms, fried with the bacon, can be added for a change.

¼ lb. macaroni or noodles, 4 eggs, ¼ lb. bacon rashers, 2 Tbs. grated cheese, ½ pint milk, salt, pepper, a little butter

Boil the pasta till tender, but not sticky, in lots of salted water. Drain, running under the hot tap for a minute to wash off excess starch. Cut the rind off the bacon and cut into strips. Fry lightly. Mix with pasta and put into a shallow oven dish. Beat up the eggs with the milk, season, add grated cheese. Pour this mixture over the pasta, dot with butter and bake in a moderate oven (gas 4, 350°F., 180°C.), for 45 minutes.

Cauliflower or spinach goes well with this.

FISH AND PASTA SALAD (*4 helpings*)

A useful pleasant way of using up leftover cooked fish. To 1 cupful of flaked cooked fish you will need roughly ¼ lb. pasta, preferably one of the decorative shell shapes. Also ¼ pint of mayonnaise into which you have stirred 1 Tbs. horseradish sauce, and some chopped fresh herbs such as tarragon, thyme, parsley. The fish should be flaked, and any skin and bones removed. Boil the pasta 12–15 minutes, until tender, drain well. Mix the herbs into the mayonnaise, add the horseradish gradually, tasting to see when it is pungent enough. When pasta is tepid, stir fish, pasta and mayonnaise together. Sprinkle with chopped parsley.

Pulses

A whole range of dried vegetables comes under this heading – haricot beans, lentils, split peas, chick peas, butter beans. They are all cheap (except the best imported lentils), can be usefully alternated with fresh vegetables, especially in winter, and form the basis of several good dishes in their own right. Incidentally, even dried vegetables deteriorate with time, so if you are stuck with a pan of beans which refuse to soften after hours of boiling, the chances are that they are antiques and have been kept too long, either in the shop, or in your own cupboard.

All these vegetables should be soaked before cooking, unless specific instructions to the contrary are given on the packet. This cuts down the cooking time considerably and makes them more tender. Soaking overnight in tepid water will be enough for all of them, except chick peas, which need 24 hours soaking and a marathon session in the cooking pot.

To cook them, drain off the water they were soaked in. Pick out any blackened-looking vegetables, and any grit which may have found its way in, add cold water to more than cover, a sliced onion, carrot, clove of garlic, salt and pepper to flavour, and bring slowly to the boil. Cover the pan and simmer till tender – which will usually take from 1–2 hours, depending on their quality and age. Split peas and lentils take less time than the others; chick peas should be boiled gently for 6 hours.

If you want to serve the pulses as they come, they are now ready to be drained and dished up with a lump of butter and a sprinkling of grated parsley or cheese stirred in. For other ideas see the following recipes.

HARICOT BEAN SALAD*

Boiled haricot beans make a pleasant salad which can be eaten on its own, as an hors d'œuvre, or with cold meat, salami, ham, etc. Allow 2 oz. beans per person.

Drain some beans, preferably while still warm, season to taste with French dressing, salt and black pepper and stir in a little finely chopped onion and parsley.

This is a handy way of using up any leftover boiled beans.

N.B. Lentils and chick peas are also good served like this. Add some garlic to the chick peas, and a little pounded anchovy to the lentils.

BRANDADE OF TUNA FISH AND HARICOT BEANS (2–3 helpings)

A Breton dish based on an unexpectedly successful combination of flavours – tuna fish, haricot beans and cheese. Apart from the preliminary soaking and boiling of the beans, the brandade is very little trouble to prepare and as it is immensely filling it only needs a green salad as accompaniment.

6–8 oz. haricot beans, 1 medium-size (approximately 6 oz.) tin of tuna fish, 3 oz. grated cheese (strong Cheddar works very well), 2 oz. butter, 1 clove garlic, 3 Tbs. fine dry breadcrumbs, salt, pepper

Soak the beans overnight. Drain. Put them in a large pan of cold water, bring to the boil slowly and cook at a moderate pace till the beans are tender – 2–3 hours, depending on the quality of the beans. Drain. The beans should be puréed, strictly speaking, which is easily done if you have a food mill but a slow business if you only have a sieve. When I am in a hurry, I find mashing them thoroughly with a fork answers quite well. Mash the tuna fish to a pulp and combine with the beans and grated cheese and half the butter. Mix well together, adding finely chopped or squeezed garlic, and salt and pepper to taste. Pile the mixture up in a buttered baking dish, strew breadcrumbs over the top and dot with butter. Bake in a hottish oven (gas 6, 400°F., 205°C.) for 20–30 minutes, or until the breadcrumbs have browned.

LENTILS AND ANCHOVIES* (*4 helpings*)

An oddly successful mixture this, with an elusive, smoky flavour, not in the least fishy. Well worth trying when you want a cheap but nourishing dish. It can be eaten on its own, with a crisp green salad and lots of black pepper, or with a halved hard-boiled egg added to each helping. The lentils must be the brown variety, which can be bought at most health food stores and good grocers.

½ lb. brown lentils, 1 onion, 1 small tin anchovy fillets, 2 cloves garlic, 3 oz. butter, salt, black pepper, 4 hard-boiled eggs (optional)

Soak the lentils in cold water for 1–2 hours. Remove any lentils and tiny stalks which float to the top. Transfer the lentils to a pan, with the roughly chopped onion, and cover with fresh cold water. Bring to the boil slowly and simmer for 1–1½ hours, till the lentils are tender but not cooked to a mush. Drain the contents of the pan in a colander. Meanwhile, pour the oil off the anchovy fillets and mash them to a pulp with a wooden spoon. Melt 1 oz. butter over low heat in a heavy pan or fire-proof serving dish (one of those shallow brown earthenware dishes would be ideal) and stir in the lentil and onion mixture, together with the garlic cloves, which can be put through the squeezer or finely minced. After a few minutes, when the lentils are heated through, stir in the pounded anchovies. Cook gently a few minutes longer, stirring in the rest of the butter, a lump at a time. Add salt and black pepper to taste. Serve, with or without the hard-boiled eggs.

This dish can be successfully re-heated by adding a little more butter and warming it, covered, in the oven for half an hour (gas 3, 325°F., 150°C.).

PEASE PUDDING* (*3–4 helpings*)

A venerable dish this, mentioned in nursery rhymes under the name of pease porridge. Traditionally served with pork in some form or other. I find it goes best with grilled or braised sausages.

1 lb. split peas, 1 onion, 1 clove, 1 carrot, 2 egg yolks, 1 oz. butter, salt and pepper

Soak the split peas overnight. Pick out any dodgy-looking ones. Put them in a pan with fresh water just to cover and the onion, with a clove stuck in it, and sliced carrot. Bring to the boil very gradually, and simmer till tender. You will probably have to add a little more *boiling* water from time to time as the peas swell and soak up their cooking water. The point of starting with less water and adding it as you go along is to prevent the peas becoming too watery, which would spoil the purée. When the peas are quite soft, rub them through a sieve with the vegetables (after removing the clove). Stir in the beaten egg yolks and a good lump of butter. Season with salt and pepper to taste. Pour the purée into a greased pudding bowl. Cover with a foil or greaseproof paper cap and steam for 30–45 minutes, standing the bowl in a pan with simmering water reaching about halfway up. The pudding should feel fairly firm. Turn it out on a dish and serve.

SPLIT PEA FRITTERS

A good way of using up any leftover pease pudding. Soften a little chopped onion in butter and mix it into the pea purée, with a bit of chopped parsley. If the purée is too soft to shape into patties, you can add a tablespoon of breadcrumbs. Now shape the mixture, which should be well seasoned, into little flat patties, brush them with beaten egg, roll in breadcrumbs and fry till golden brown.

These are immensely filling. You could use them to round out a dish of bacon and eggs. Or they go well with strongly spiced Continental boiling sausage.

CHICK PEAS CATALAN (*4–6 helpings*)

Chick peas have a nutty flavour quite unlike any other dried vegetable. The Spanish make great use of them in stews and casserole dishes, together with chorizos (highly spiced sausages), odd bits of meat or game, herbs, wine and lots of garlic. This is an adaptation of a Catalan dish. Some delicatessen shops, particularly round Soho, stock real chorizos, but any highly spiced Continental boiling sausage could be substituted.

1 lb. chick peas, 1 large onion, 1 carrot, 1 stalk celery, 1 bacon bone with trimmings, 1 sausage, bunch of herbs (parsley,

thyme, bayleaf, garlic), $\frac{1}{2}$ pint tomato sauce (*see* p. 41) or 1 small tin tomato purée, garlic and parsley for garnish, salt, pepper

Soak the chick peas for 24 hours, or longer. Put them in plenty of fresh water in a large pan with the onion, sliced carrot and celery. Push the bacon bone down among the peas, together with the herbs, parcelled with a length of cotton. Add 2 Tbs. oil to the cooking water. Bring the contents of the pan slowly to the boil, skimming if necessary, and boil steadily over lowest heat for 2 hours. Add the sausage. Cook for a further 2–3 hours, or until the peas are tender. Now pour the stock off into a bowl, remove the herbs, and transfer the peas, bacon, etc., to a casserole. If you are using tomato sauce, dilute it with enough of the cooking liquid to cover the peas. If you are using purée, mix the contents of the tin with the stock thoroughly and adjust seasoning. Pour the liquid over the peas, mixing well. Continue cooking, covered, on top of the stove over low heat for 1–2 hours longer. Alternatively, put the dish, covered, into a moderate oven (gas 3, 325°F., 150°C.) for about the same length of time. If the dish seems to be getting too dry, add any remaining stock from the peas or a little boiling water. Quarter of an hour before serving stir in the finely chopped garlic and parsley and 1 Tbs. olive oil.

Serve with the sausage cut into chunks, the bacon removed from the bone. Thick rounds of French bread moistened with a little olive oil, salt and crushed garlic would be appropriate with this dish.

SHORT CRUST PASTRY

Making pastry is one of those things which seems dishearteningly complicated if you have never tried it, and childishly simple once you have. Short crust pastry, particularly, is quick and easy to make, versatile and reasonably foolproof – no pastry, as expert cooks will corroborate, is one hundred per cent foolproof. On the other hand, if you stick to the directions, it will always be edible even if it falls short of crisp perfection.

Many cookbook recipes for pastry making are bogged down in theory. The more confidently you tackle it, I find, the better it turns out (your hands are likely to be cooler for one thing) so I shall give the instructions first and diagnose briefly a few of the things that can go wrong afterwards.

To line one 8–9 inch flan case or cover an average-sized pie dish you will need:

6 oz. plain flour, 3½ oz. butter, 1 egg yolk, 1–2 Tbs. water, pinch salt, squeeze lemon juice, 1 level Tbs. sugar as well if the pie is to have a sweet filling

1. Sift flour, salt, and sugar if you are using it, together into a large mixing bowl.
2. Make a well in the centre. Put in the butter and start cutting it into the flour with a knife. The idea is to break the butter up small while working in as much flour as possible. When the knife seems to have done what it can, use your fingertips to rub the mixture together till the butter has absorbed all the loose flour and the particles are the size of breadcrumbs (fresh not dried crumbs). *Don't* overdo this stage to be on the safe side – pastry is better handled too little than too much.
3. Beat up egg yolk with the water and stir into the crumbs with your knife. Add a squeeze of lemon juice to make the dough more pliable.
4. Gather the sticky mess together with your fingertips and work lightly till it sticks together in a lump and some of the stickiness has gone.

Now put it on a plate in a cool place, or in the fridge, to rest for an hour or two before use. The point of this is to make the dough less tough and less liable to shrink in cooking.

To roll the dough out, flour the table top and the rolling pin (or milk bottle), and dust a little flour over the lump of pastry itself if it still feels very sticky. Roll out lightly but firmly till it is just under ¼ inch thick. If holes appear tear off a patch, moisten the edges with milk and iron over the hole with your pin, sprinkling on a little more flour. Now lift the pastry sheet gently off the table – I usually slide a long knife blade underneath because some bit often sticks. Lay it over the flan tin, ease it in to fit the tin with your fingertips, taking care not to stretch it. Press it firmly down once it is in place – if you grease the tin lightly first the pastry will stick more obediently. Prick the bottom here and there with a fork. Run the pin over the top of the tin to trim off overhang.

The next stage depends on whether your pastry is to cook with the filling, or separately. If the former, it is ready for the filling. If the latter (this is called baking 'blind') cut a circle or strips of greaseproof paper to cover the bottom. Then put in a cup of uncooked haricot beans. (Rice or crusts will do if you have no beans.) Put the flan in the top part of a pre-heated oven (gas 6, 400°F., 205°C.) and bake 20 minutes. Remove paper and beans and return to oven for another 5–7 minutes. The pastry shell will now be golden brown, crisp and ready either to take a hot filling or can be left to cool and stored in an airtight tin.

Some recipes only require the pastry to be partly pre-baked, in which case you can dispense with the beans and paper.

If you are using the pastry to *cover* a pie, roll it out a little thicker, put an eggcup in the pie dish to support the pastry (if the area is fairly large), and make a few slashes in the pastry to let out steam. The pie will look more elegant if you cut a long strip of pastry, moisten it on both sides with milk or water, and press it round the rim of the pie dish, before laying on the pastry cover. You can then go round the edge with a fork, dipped in milk, to give a ribbed effect and press the two layers firmly together. Odd bits of pastry can be cut into flower and leaf shapes and stuck over the pie with a spot of milk. Brush over the whole surface with milk or beaten egg yolk to colour it attractively and bake as directed.

Notes

1. The recipe given above is for a rich short crust. For greater economy you can use half butter half margarine, all margarine, or half butter half lard. Some people swear by the one, some by the other, but I think butter tastes nicer and the extra cost is negligible. For eating cold, however, margarine makes a lighter-textured pastry. You can dispense with the egg yolk, in which case use a *little* more water.

2. If the pastry comes out hard and tough you used too much water. If it is crumbly too much fat. If soggy, it has had too much handling or been cooked initially at too low a temperature. Pre-heating the oven is important.

3. If things *still* go wrong, check that you are making pastry under the right conditions – everything, from room temperature to your hands, should be as cool as possible. Cool your hands by rinsing under a cold tap and drying, and make the pastry if possible in the morning before the kitchen heats up. Above all don't worry – try it a couple more times and it will come right.

ALSATIAN ONION TART* (*2–4 helpings*)

An excellent recipe for the end of the week, when you are running out of cash and/or ideas. All you need is lots of onions, butter, short crust pastry and a couple of eggs. The filling is very tasty and the tart can be eaten hot, lukewarm or cold.

Line your flan tin with short crust pastry. Peel and chop 2 lb. onions (you can make do with less) and cook them over a low heat with just enough water in the pan to stop them burning. When they are soft and tender, add a generous lump of butter and leave to stew a few minutes longer. Then take them off the heat and add just enough flour to bind them (1–2 Tbs.), salt, black pepper, 2 beaten eggs and, if possible 1 Tbs. cream or top of milk, to make a thick mush. Spread this onion mixture in the flan tin, spoon a little more cream (grated cheese could be used) over the top and bake in a fairly hot oven (gas 7, 425°F.,

220°C.) for 20 minutes, then lower the heat a couple of notches and continue cooking till the pastry is crisp and the top nicely browned, ¾–1 hour.

A plain green salad goes well with this. No other vegetables.

CABBAGE KOULIBIAC (*3–4 helpings*)

A humble version of the famous koulibiac of salmon, but very good provided the pastry is crisp and the cabbage and hard-boiled egg filling is tender and savoury. Green Savoy cabbage is best, but any type can be used if you parboil it till tender first.

1 lb. cabbage, 2 onions, 4 hard-boiled eggs, 1 tsp. dill, fennel or caraway seed, 3 oz. butter, a little sour cream or yoghourt, 8 oz. short crust pastry, salt, black pepper

Quarter cabbage, and parboil for approximately five minutes or till just tender. Drain, then squeeze in your hands to get out as much moisture as possible. Peel, finely chop onions. Fry them in the butter gently. Chop cabbage roughly and add to the onions, with the herb seed. Add salt and black pepper. Stir thoroughly to mix, then leave to cool for half an hour. Roll the short crust pastry (*see* p. 100) thinly on a floured surface to make a rectangle roughly 12 × 8 inches. Peel and chop hard-boiled eggs, and scatter half of this over the middle of the pastry. Stir cream or yoghourt into the cabbage, pile on top of the egg, and finish with another sprinkle of chopped egg. Bring sides of pastry up over the filling and pinch together to make a fat bolster shape. Pinch ends shut too. Brush pastry with milk, then put in a fairly hot oven (gas 6, 400°F., 200°C.) and cook for ten minutes, then turn down to gas 5, 375°F., 200°C. and cook for another twenty minutes, or till pastry is crisp and golden brown.

Just before serving open up the top and pour in a little butter melted with a dash of lemon juice. Good with boiled buttered carrots or a beetroot salad.

APPLE CHEESECAKE (*4–6 helpings*)

This is made without cheese, but the taste oddly resembles the classic cheesecake, though the general effect is lighter and more refreshing.

Short crust pastry flan case, 5 cooking apples, 2 egg yolks, grated rind of 1 lemon, 1 oz. softened butter, 2 Tbs. dry breadcrumbs, sugar

Pre-bake the pastry for 15 minutes in a brisk oven (gas 7, 425°F., 220°C.). Peel, core and stew the apples in very little water with 1 Tbs. sugar, over low heat, stirring to prevent the mixture catching and burning. Sieve the apples and stir in melted butter and lemon rind. When the mixture has cooled slightly, add the beaten egg yolks. Pour into the pastry case and sprinkle the top with breadcrumbs. Bake in a moderate oven (gas 4, 350°F., 180°C.) till the top has browned and the filling feels set when you press it lightly with a finger, about 30–45 minutes.

SUET CRUST

Suet crust is made in much the same way as short crust, using beef suet instead of butter or margarine. One useful point about it is that it can be used either for steamed puddings, like the steak and kidney pudding, or baked as in jam roly-poly. Properly made, it is light and melting, quite unlike the soggy blanket characteristic of canteen cookery. It would be a pity if the new generation of cooks ignored it, because it is associated with some of the best traditional English dishes.

To make enough dough to line a 1½ pint pudding basin you will need:
½ lb. self-raising flour or ½ lb. plain flour plus 1 tsp. baking-powder, ¼ lb. grated beef suet, pinch of salt, water to mix. For an extra light, spongy dough replace 2 oz. flour with 2 oz. fresh

white breadcrumbs. For a sweet pudding, mix in ½ Tbs. white or brown sugar.

Sift flour, salt and sugar together. Add the suet, rubbing in lightly with the fingertips for a minute. Add enough water to make a light, spongy dough. Knead this lightly into a smooth ball on a floured board, roll out and use at once.

BAKED APPLE PUDDING* (*3 helpings*)

Suet crust, as in previous recipe, 1¼ lb. apples, 2 oz. butter, ¼ lb. soft brown sugar, juice 2 lemons and a little grated rind, 2 Tbs. water

Cream the butter, lemon juice and brown sugar together and put it in the bottom of a greased pudding basin. Roll out the crust and line the bottom and sides, covering the butter/sugar, and leaving an overhang round the sides. Peel, core and slice the apples and lay them, together with the grated lemon rind and water, on the crust. Fold over the edges to cover, and seal. Bake the pudding in a fairly hot oven (gas 6, 375°F., 190°C.) till brown, then lower heat (gas 2, 275°F., 140°C.) to finish cooking, which will take about 2 hours in all.

To serve, turn the pudding out on to a plate. The sugar and butter mixture will have turned to a lemony sauce which runs out over the top of the pudding.

Serve with more sugar and cream.

BAKED ROLY-POLY* (*4–6 helpings*)

You can either use the recipe for suet crust on p. 105 or the one given here, which makes use of breadcrumbs.

6 oz. self-raising flour, or plain flour plus pinch baking powder, 2 oz. fresh white breadcrumbs, 5 oz. chopped beef suet, ½ Tbs. Demerara sugar, jam or marmalade

Make the suet crust as described on p. 105, adding crumbs after the suet. Roll it out to a strip about 7 or 8 inches wide. Spread thickly with slightly warmed jam – plum, apricot, cherry or home-made marmalade are best. Roll up. Press the edges lightly together. Butter one side of a baking tin only. Lay your roll in the angle of the tin, and put something under the other side to keep it tilted – this will stop the pudding spreading uncontrollably while cooking. Bake in a moderate oven (gas 5, 375°F., 190°C.) for 30–45 minutes.

Serve this either just as it is, or with a little more jam diluted with water, heated and dished up as a sauce.

Batter

All the dishes using batter, from fritters to Yorkshire pudding one tends to enjoy very much when made by someone else, but lazily avoid making oneself. This is a pity because batter is one of the small miracles of cookery – how that pallid liquid is metamorphosed into a puffy golden pillow-crust is a mystery I hope never to have explained to me.

As sheer padding, batter is unbeatable value. Try the toad-in-the-hole recipe and see. Alternatively, 1 aubergine, cut into thin slices (sweated for an hour or more, sprinkled with salt) and then dipped into batter and fried will make enough fritters for four or more people.

As I have given the batter-making procedure in some detail in the recipe for Toad-in-the-Hole I will not go into it here. A point to keep in mind when making batter, though: always bring it into contact with strong heat – whether you are baking it in the oven, or frying it in deep fat. (Fritters can be fried in shallow fat but not so successfully.) This makes it light and ungreasy. In the case of fritters drain them on crumpled paper for a minute before eating. If you wish, you may allow the batter to stand for an hour or so before using.

TOAD-IN-THE-HOLE* (*4 helpings*)

Not a dish for sophisticates but an excellent way of stretching half a pound of chipolatas into a solid meal for four people. Children, especially, love it. If you have time I suggest braising the sausages for ¾ hour in a moderate oven (gas 4, 325°F., 150°C.) with a little stock, gravy or butter and a dash of Worcestershire Sauce, to encourage them to sweat out some of their lye, and remove that raw pink appearance. Drain them on kitchen tissue to remove excess fat.

¼ lb. flour, ½ lb. skinless pork chipolatas, 2 eggs, ½ pint milk, salt, a little dripping or butter

To make the batter, sieve the flour and a pinch of salt into a large mixing bowl. Make a well in the middle, so that the bottom of the bowl is exposed. Break the eggs into this well and stir a little milk into them with a wooden spoon, delicately at first to avoid mixing in the flour. Then gradually begin incorporating the flour, adding a little more milk as you go along. Go on stirring in the flour and adding small quantities of milk till the mixture is the consistency of cream. At this point you can beat the mixture thoroughly with an egg whisk. After a minute or two, if you wish, put the batter aside to stand for an hour.

Now heat the butter or dripping in the baking tin, pour in the batter, drop the sausages in here and there, and bake for 35 minutes in a brisk oven (gas 7, 425°F., 220°C.).

N.B. It is important to have the baking tin and oven well heated. A warm tin, or cool oven, will stop the batter rising.

If you have not experimented with batters before you will be agreeably surprised by the transformation of the anaemic-looking raw batter into a billowing golden puff reminiscent of the best Yorkshire puddings. An unsophisticated vegetable should accompany this dish – boiled, buttered cabbage or sprouts.

YORKSHIRE PUDDING★ (*4 helpings*)

Almost everyone likes a good Yorkshire pudding, and it is easier to make than those flabby slices served up with institutional meals would lead you expect. From the economy point of view, a generous helping of Yorkshire pudding will make people less greedy for roast beef.

½ pint milk, ¼ lb. flour, 2 eggs, pinch salt

Put the sifted flour into a bowl, make a well in the centre and add milk gradually, beating hard. Then add eggs, beating hard after each one. Add pinch of salt. Put into the fridge, or in a cool place, until 35 minutes before the roast has finished cooking. Pour half the fat from the roasting tin into another baking tin (or cake tin). Make it smoking hot over the fire and then pour in the batter. Cook the pudding at the top of the oven (gas 6, 400°F., 205°C.) for 30–35 minutes, or until puffy and golden on top. The roast has to be moved down to a lower shelf to finish cooking.

PANCAKES★

Pancakes sprinkled with brown sugar and lemon juice, or filled with apricot jam, are an almost irresistible pudding. They are not difficult to make unless you are aiming for perfect circles, in which case you will need a cast-iron pan made specially for the purpose, straight-sided, like the ones used in Brittany, where pancakes are a local speciality. An ordinary medium-sized heavyweight frying pan gives less immaculate results, but the taste, after all, is the same.

Pancake batter is made like ordinary batter except that you add a little melted butter halfway. *See* Toad-in-the-Hole (p. 108) for instructions.

For 8 medium-sized pancakes you need 4 oz. plain flour,

1 dessertspoon caster sugar, $\frac{1}{2}$ oz. or more melted butter, pinch of salt, 1 egg and 1 yolk, approximately $\frac{1}{2}$ pint milk

Proceed as for Toad-in-the-Hole until you have stirred in about half the milk and the batter is a thickish cream. Now stir in the butter, melted in a cup over hot water and left to cool a bit. Stir in more milk till the batter is a *thin* cream and, if you wish, leave to stand in a cool place for an hour or so. Now heat your pan slowly till it is good and hot and with a pad of kitchen tissue sprinkled with a little vegetable oil (you can use melted butter but oil is better because it doesn't burn and is tasteless) wipe a film of oil over the pan. The idea of greasing the pan is to prevent the batter sticking, *not* in any sense to fry the pancake. Then take a generous Tbs. of batter, drop it into the pan and immediately shake the pan gently with a clockwise turn of the wrist to spread the batter thinly over the bottom. As soon as the pancake edges can be easily detached the pancake is ready to be turned over. Traditionally you should toss it, which needs a strong wrist and an accurate eye. If tennis was not your strong suit, work a metal slice or spatula under the pancake and flip it over rapidly to brown the other side. As they are done, stack them on a plate in the oven, which should be warm, not hot. And that's all there is to it.

N.B. For a change you can try folding the beaten leftover egg white into your batter. This gives a fluffier-textured pancake. You can also vary the flavour of the batter itself by adding a little vanilla, grated lemon peel, or even a spoonful of brandy or rum if you happen to have such a thing. And the choice of fillings is enormous: apple purée, sultanas soaked in lemon juice and beaten into sweetened cream cheese, chopped walnuts and brown sugar, redcurrant jelly, to suggest only a few.

NORMANDY APPLE FRITTERS (*4 helpings*)

4 large cooking apples, $\frac{1}{2}$ pint cider, 4 oz. flour, pinch of salt, 3 Tbs. oil or melted butter, 1 egg white, pinch cinnamon, 1 lemon, 4 Tbs. sugar

The batter may be made several hours before using, or the night before. Mix the flour in a bowl with oil or melted butter and pinch of salt and gradually add 6 fl. oz. cider, stirring well with a wooden spoon till the batter is smooth and runny. The stiffly beaten egg white is stirred into the batter just before using it.

The apples should be prepared about an hour in advance. Peel and core them, leaving them whole, and slice into $\frac{1}{2}$ inch rings. Put the rings in a bowl and pour over them a marinade made from the remaining cider, juice of the lemon, pinch of cinnamon and 2 Tbs. sugar. Turn the rings over to make sure they are all moistened with the liquid.

A deep fryer is the ideal thing for cooking fritters but you could make do with a saucepan. What you must have is plenty of oil – $1\frac{1}{2}$ pints to 1 quart of corn or vegetable oil, which is practically tasteless. Heat the oil good and hot. Meanwhile, shake excess marinade off the apple rings, wiping them with tissue, stir beaten egg white into the batter and put a large plate with a couple of layers of kitchen tissue ready for the fritters. Heat the oven to gas 4, 350°F., 180°C. When the oil is ready (this is never easy to gauge but an experimental fritter can be dropped in to test it – it should be hot enough to seal the batter immediately, and your fritter should take approximately 2 minutes to cook) dip the apple rings in the batter and then drop them quickly into the oil. You will be able to fry three or four at once. As soon as they look puffy and golden brown, lift them out with a perforated spoon, lay them on the paper in the large dish, sprinkle sugar over and put them into the oven while you do the next batch. Watch to see that the oil does not get too hot or the batter will turn dark brown before the apple ring has cooked. In this case reduce the heat a little. When the fritters are all ready, remove the paper, strew more sugar over them and serve at once, either just as they are or with thin cream.

Soufflé Mixtures

I have given detailed instructions on preparing and cooking a soufflé on p. 124 in the Fast Work chapter, so I won't go over the same ground here. Using the same basic soufflé mixture as for the salmon soufflé – ¼ pint white sauce, 3 egg yolks, 4 beaten whites – and adding different flavouring ingredients, you can produce a wide range of soufflés, savoury and sweet. These quantities will make a main dish for two, or a first course for three or four people. The following are a few suggested variations on the soufflé theme, which are both cheap and easy to do.

CHEESE SOUFFLÉ

¼ pint white sauce (made with ¼ pint milk, 1 level dessertspoon flour, 1 oz. butter), 3 egg yolks, 4 whites, 3 oz. grated cheese, pinch dry mustard, salt, pepper, paprika or cayenne to taste

Make White Sauce as described on p. 43. Cool slightly then beat in egg yolks, mustard, salt, pepper and cayenne or paprika. Stir in the grated cheese (Parmesan, Gruyère, Cheshire, Double Gloucester or plain Cheddar) and mix well. Then fold in egg whites, stiffly beaten, and turn the mixture into a buttered dish. Bake in hottish oven (gas 6, 400°F., 205°C.) for 20 minutes, if you like soufflés a little runny in the middle, 4–5 minutes longer if you prefer them dry. Serve at once.

SPINACH SOUFFLÉ

¼ pint white sauce, 3 yolks, 4 egg whites, 1 lb. spinach, 1–2 oz. grated cheese, salt, pepper, nutmeg, 1–2 Tbs. cream or top of milk

The spinach should be washed, cooked in water left on the leaves from washing, and then sieved to a purée. Add 4 Tbs. of this purée to the basic white sauce, together with the cream or top of milk, salt, pepper and a grating of nutmeg. Simmer for a few minutes. Remove from heat and cool a little before beating in the yolks and grated cheese. Fold in whites and proceed as for Cheese Soufflé (*see* p. 112).

BLACK TREACLE SOUFFLÉ (*4 helpings*)

An original and distinguished soufflé to which the treacle (or blackstrap molasses) gives a rich, dark-brown sort of taste. Don't expect it to set firm, the bottom stays a bit gooey. Good with thin plain cream.

2 oz. butter, 2 oz. plain flour, $\frac{1}{2}$ pint milk, 3 Tbs. black treacle or molasses, $\frac{1}{2}$ tsp. each of nutmeg, cinnamon and ginger, pinch salt, 4 eggs, 2 Tbs. sugar

Make your basic soufflé mixture by melting butter, stirring in flour, then adding milk and stirring till thick and smooth, but not too stiff. Remove from heat, and stir in treacle, spices and salt. Let cool for a few minutes. Beat egg yolks till frothy, with the sugar, then stir into the treacle mixture, mixing well. Beat egg whites and fold into the soufflé mixture gently but thoroughly. Turn into an oiled 8-inch soufflé dish and set the dish in a pan of hot water – water should come about half way up the soufflé. Bake in moderate oven (gas 5, 365°F., 195°C.) for about three-quarters of an hour. It should have a spongy texture on top, with a creamy one at the bottom.

CHOCOLATE SOUFFLÉ

To make this 2–2$\frac{1}{2}$ oz. plain chocolate should be added to the previous mixture, and 2 oz. vanilla sugar should be used but no vanilla essence.

To add the chocolate, grate the piece of chocolate into a pan with 1–2 Tbs. water and stir over very low heat till soft. Heat milk separately and mix with the melted chocolate gradually, stirring well till smooth. In another pan stir the flour into 1 Tbs. cold milk, and add a little of the hot milk/chocolate to this paste. When thoroughly combined pour in the rest of the chocolate-flavoured milk and continue cooking, adding vanilla sugar and tiny pinch salt, till the mixture has thickened. Proceed as for vanilla soufflé.

Nice eaten with thin cream.

Breadcrumbs

Two sorts of breadcrumbs are extensively used in cooking – dried crumbs for coating* food for frying, or sprinkling on top of various dishes cooked uncovered in the oven, and fresh crumbs for making various stuffings, dumpling mixtures, bread sauce, etc.

Dried crumbs are made by putting ends of loaves, crusts, leftover slices, etc., in a baking tin at the bottom of the oven to dry out while you are cooking other dishes. When they are dry they are crushed, the easiest way is to wrap them in a cloth and roll them with a rolling pin, put through a coarse sieve, and then store in a screwtop jar. They will keep for several weeks, if you remember to put the lid back at once after use. You *can* buy dry crumbs ready-made, but these look and taste odd, and the extra expense hardly seems justified when you can make your own easily and economically with odd bits of bread.

Fresh or soft breadcrumbs are made by rubbing white bread through a sieve or a grater. The bread should be a day old at

*In case you were wondering, this is done for a reason, not merely for decoration. The breadcrumbs form a protective coating over the food which seals in the flavour and juices, and in the case of the fried food, is lighter and less greasy than batter.

least, and you should not use the crusts. If you are making a stuffing in a tremendous hurry you can tear the bread up with your fingertips, but the result will be lumpier. Incidentally, fresh crumbs will not keep – they go mouldy in a trice – so you have to make them afresh each time.

CLAUDIA'S DUMPLINGS★ (*4 helpings*)

Most stews and casseroles, and many soups, are improved by the addition of stodge in one form or another. As a change from potatoes, pasta or rice, these Austrian bread dumplings are worth a try. Unlike the flour or suet variety, which are apt to taste like rubber and weight the stomach like lead shot, these are light and digestible.

6 slices from a white sandwich loaf, a little milk, 1 egg, 1 large onion, 2–3 rashers bacon, 1 Tbs. herbs (parsley, thyme, marjoram, sage), salt, pepper

Remove crusts and soak the bread in milk till soft. Squeeze out as much milk as possible. Chop onion finely. Cut off rind and snip bacon into small pieces with scissors. Fry bacon in its own fat, with the chopped onion, till the bacon is cooked and the onion golden. Mix all the ingredients together in a bowl; bind with the beaten egg and add salt and pepper to taste. Form the mixture into balls, $1\frac{1}{2}$–2 inches in diameter, if they are to be eaten with, or in, a stew, goulash or casserole, and rather smaller if they are to be added to soup. Boil up a large pan of salted water and drop the dumplings in. Cover. Reduce heat to a moderate boil and cook for about 20 minutes.

Yeast Dough and Pizza

Though serious baking and bread-making is probably too much of a performance for most people, it is well worth learning how to make a simple yeast dough so as to be able to turn out your own pizza. A pizza (plural, pizze), in case you have not encountered one, is an Italian classic, a foundation of white bread dough baked with a savoury topping which usually includes chopped tomatoes, anchovy fillets, herbs like oregano and basil, and melted cheese. Preparing the dough sounds more alarming than it is – my first attempt was perfectly successful. Once you have got that part of it taped, the rest takes no time at all, and the dish looks as good as it tastes. An extra large pizza, made with 3 times the quantities given below, and baked on a baking sheet, would be an easy and economical lunch or supper dish for six people, eaten with a large salad and, if possible, plenty of rough red wine.

PIZZA (*2 helpings*)

6 oz. plain flour, a little over $\frac{1}{4}$ oz. baker's yeast (I find this equals $1\frac{1}{2}$ level tsp. of the active baking yeast as sold in packets), a little tepid water, salt, 6–8 fresh tomatoes or 1 medium tin peeled tomatoes, 10 anchovy fillets, 4 oz. cheese (preferably Gruyère or Bel Paese but Cheddar will do), a few chopped spring onions or 2 finely chopped garlic cloves, sprinkling of oregano, basil, seasoning, olive oil

Put the yeast into a few Tbs. of tepid water to dissolve for 10–15 minutes. Sift flour and a good pinch of salt into a warmed basin. Make a well in the centre, pour in the yeast, fold the flour over the top and mix well. Add enough tepid water, $\frac{1}{8}$–$\frac{1}{4}$ pint, to make a stiff dough. Put this on a floured board and knead it for several minutes, holding the ball of dough firm with one hand and pressing it away from you with the other, rather as if you were stretching out a length of elastic. After about 5 minutes of this you will find the dough has changed consistency and become smooth, fine grained and quite a bit lighter. The point of kneading is to distribute the yeast – the raising agent – evenly throughout the dough. Roll the dough into a ball, put it on a large well-floured plate, cover it with a clean dish cloth, and put it in a warm draughtless place to rise for 2½–3 hours. (A sheltered corner near the stove or a radiator, or better still, an airing cupboard.) By now the dough should have doubled in volume. It is a good idea to have the ingredients for the topping prepared in the meantime, because the quicker you get your dough into the oven the better.

For the topping you need to peel and roughly chop the tomatoes, if you are using fresh ones, or drain off the liquid, if you are using tinned tomatoes. The cheese should be cut into thin shavings, the spring onions chopped into rounds, or the garlic finely chopped.

Now roll out the dough to about ¼ inch thick on a floured surface. You can either cook it as one large pizza on a baking sheet, or divide it into two discs, cooked separately in flan tins. In either case sprinkle a little oil over the sheet or tins, lay the pizza on top, spread the surface quickly with the tomato and onion or garlic. Lay the anchovy fillets here and there on top, sprinkle herbs, salt and pepper over, and finally the cheese (unless you are using Bel Paese, which melts so rapidly it should be added only a few minutes before the pizza has finished cooking). Dribble a little oil over the top of the pizza, or pizze, transfer quickly to a hot oven (gas 8, 450°F., 230°C.) and bake for 20–30 minutes, depending on the size of the pizza. Eat it at once, because the dough gets rubbery when cold.

You can vary the topping by adding a few black olives, strips of ham or sliced mushrooms softened in a little oil.

SEMOLINA GNOCCHI (*3–4 helpings*)

The only form in which I have ever liked semolina is as gnocchi, an Italian dish which combines semolina, Parmesan, nutmeg, eggs and milk into a delicious, golden, slightly crumbly substance which can be eaten as a dish on its own, or together with a rich stew, or roast chicken, or anything you fancy. I must point out, though, that even Italians find gnocchi temperamental to produce successfully. The semolina must be fresh, likewise the Parmesan. If you have a good Italian delicatessen or grocer's shop locally where they will provide both, gnocchi are well worth trying – otherwise you are liable to produce something like a flabby cheese pudding.

1 pint milk, 4 oz. medium-grain semolina, 4 oz. grated Parmesan, 2 eggs, salt, pepper, nutmeg, 1 oz. butter

In the top of a double boiler heat the milk to boiling point. Gradually pour in the semolina, stirring all the time, add a pinch of salt, grating of nutmeg and dusting of black pepper and continue cooking and stirring till the mixture is very thick and stiff. Remove from fire. Beat up the eggs and mix them thoroughly, together with 3 oz. of the grated Parmesan, into the semolina mixture. Pour out the mixture on to a lightly oiled flat tin or baking sheet, in a layer about $\frac{1}{2}$ inch thick. Leave to get cold.

Ten minutes or so before you want to eat the gnocchi, cut the cold semolina mixture into squares or rounds, lay them in a fireproof dish, sprinkle over the rest of the Parmesan and dot with plenty of butter (1 oz. or more). Put the dish in a hot oven (gas 7, 425°F., 220°C.) for 5–8 minutes, or until the gnocchi are warmed through and the cheese and butter melted and slightly browned.

If you are in a hurry, you can put the cheese and butter straight over the uncut gnocchi in the tin.

Fast Work

This is the chapter for evenings when you get back late from work, with two people expected for supper, or when a long car journey leaves everyone clamouring for immediate sustenance, or when you want a rapid but not skimpy meal after a late show – in fact for any of the occasions when a meal has to be prepared at the double, with materials to hand. Many of the recipes make use of tinned foods, for convenience, but not too obviously – presumably no one needs advice on how to prepare baked beans on toast, and besides this is probably not what hungry people would consider a meal. Maximum preparation and cooking time is never more than an hour and, in most cases, considerably less. I have given the stages of preparation in some detail, to avoid fuss and fluster, and if you follow them carefully you should be able to produce a very presentable meal for two to four people – soup, main dish and even a pudding – in an hour, without becoming dishevelled, tired and irritable in the process.

This sort of cooking does require some forethought. You should keep a selection of tins on hand, as well as quite a few spices and herbs to ginger them up, and you will need the usual standbys – milk, eggs, butter, bread. For real emergencies, when the cupboard is practically bare, I have included one or two snack ideas at the end of the chapter.

QUICK ONION SOUP (*4 helpings*)

The touch of inspiration in this recipe, given to me by a French friend, is the caramelizing of the onions which gives the soup colour, body and a rich but delicate flavour all at once.

4 large onions, 1 oz. butter, $\frac{1}{2}$ Tbs. sugar, $1\frac{3}{4}$ pints water and bouillon cube, a dash of wine vinegar

Slice the onions thinly. Melt 1 oz. butter in a large frying pan, put in the onions. Stir them around till they begin to go soft, then put in the sugar. Keep stirring till the sugar browns – brown *not* black – and then pour in the hot water and bouillon cube, and a dash of vinegar. Simmer for $\frac{1}{4}$ hour, taste and add salt and pepper if necessary.

Serve plain with buttered toast.

GARLIC SOUP* (*4 helpings*)

The Spanish call this sopa de ajo and consume it in great quantities, believing, as they do, that some garlic a day keeps the doctor away. It is very easy to make, costs practically nothing, and is good – if you like garlic.

6 cloves garlic, 1 pint water, salt, 2 eggs, 1 Tbs. butter or oil

Peel 6 cloves of garlic, removing any green shoots they may have sprouted as this makes them bitter. Chop roughly and colour gently over a low flame in 1 Tbs. butter or a little oil. Pour on 1 pint boiling water and cook for 15 minutes.

Separate yolks and whites of 2 eggs. Poach the whites in the soup, strain and set aside on a warm plate. Beat up the egg yolks and pour the soup little by little on to them (you can strain it at this stage if you think actual *lumps* of garlic would be too much) stirring vigorously. Taste, and season with pepper and salt. Put the soup back over a low flame for a minute to warm up, *not* boil, which would scramble your eggs. Put a few fingers of bread or a slice of French loaf into each bowl, place a bit of the poached white on top, pour the soup over and serve.

CHINESE EGG DROP SOUP (*2 helpings*)

1 pint stock, ¼ lb. mushrooms, handful watercress or spring onions, 1 dessertspoon soya sauce, 1 egg

Chop mushrooms and cress or spring onions roughly and simmer in stock still tender. Add soya sauce. Beat egg in a cup and stir it rapidly through the bubbling soup till it forms yellow strands. Serve at once.

CURRIED BAKED EGGS (*2–3 helpings*)

Quickly made, and surprisingly filling.

4 hard-boiled eggs, 2 raw eggs, 1 oz. butter, 1 scant tsp. curry powder, salt, cayenne pepper, home-made toasted breadcrumbs

Butter a small fireproof dish. Slice hard-boiled eggs and arrange in layers in dish. Whisk two remaining eggs with salt, cayenne, curry powder and pour over the sliced egg. Strew the top with breadcrumbs, dot with more butter and bake for ten minutes at gas 7, 425°F., 220°C. When the top feels firm the dish is done.

EGGS IN CHEESE SAUCE* (*main dish for 2, or first course for 4*)

Like the Eggs in Onion Sauce on p. 44 this is a much more sustaining dish than it sounds. If it is to be the main dish I suggest serving it on a bed of puréed spinach – the slight bitterness tones down the richness of the sauce. You can use more or less eggs according to your appetite.

6 eggs, 1 pint milk, 1 Tbs. butter, 1 Tbs. flour, ¼ lb. Cheddar, nutmeg, salt, pepper, mustard

Start with the sauce. Melt 1 rounded Tbs. butter, stir in 1 rounded Tbs. flour, pour on 1 pint cold milk and bring to boil over moderate heat. Put on pan of water and add eggs just before the water boils to reduce the risk of cracking. Cook them for just over 5 minutes. Grate the cheese. Reduce heat to simmering point when the sauce boils. In a minute or two, it will thicken considerably. Now add grated cheese, stirring for a minute or so till it melts. When the eggs are done, pour off water, run cold water over them, and crack the shells to stop them cooking away in their own heat. Taste the sauce and add salt, pepper, a dusting of nutmeg and ½ tsp. mustard for pungency.

Peel the eggs, halve them and arrange them flat side down in a shallow heatproof dish (flan tin at a pinch). If you are using spinach, spoon the hot purée into a dish and arrange the eggs on top. Pour the sauce over the eggs and brown lightly under a hot grill.

TORTILLA (*2 helpings*)

A Spanish omelette, or tortilla, is a solid, rustic dish compared with its French equivalent. The eggs feature as a binding for the other ingredients, which can be varied according to what you have to hand – diced green pepper, rounds of sausage, bits of kidney, chicken, ham. But remember all the ingredients must be cooked before adding the eggs.

2 medium-sized boiled potatoes, 2 onions, 2 cloves garlic, 4 eggs, salt, pepper, butter or oil, a little parsley

Chop onions roughly and fry in a little olive oil, or oil and butter, till golden. Add peeled diced potato, and chopped garlic, and fry over moderate heat till the potatoes are lightly browned. Beat up eggs with salt and pepper to taste, stir in finely chopped parsley, and pour over the contents of the pan, shaking to distribute them evenly. After 3 or 4 minutes put the pan under a moderate grill to cook the top of the tortilla, which should be well set but not burnt. If it looks dry dot with a little butter before serving.

A tomato and onion salad goes well with tortilla.

Wedges of cold tortilla sandwiched in crusty rolls are a popular picnic food in Spain.

POACHED EGGS ON CREAMED PEAS (*2 helpings*)

This recipe shows what a little ingenuity can produce from the standard café offering of bacon, eggs and peas.

1 large packet frozen peas, 4 eggs, 1 Tbs. vinegar, 4 rashers streaky bacon, 1 slice bread, 1 oz. butter, 2–3 Tbs. cream or top of milk, salt, sugar, pepper

Boil the peas in a little water till tender. Drain and sieve into a shallow oven dish. Stir in butter, 2 Tbs. cream, pinch sugar and a little salt and pepper. Put the dish to keep warm in a low oven (gas 1, 275°F., 140°C.). Half fill a frying pan with water, to which you have added 1 Tbs. vinegar, and heat till the water is simmering. Break in the eggs carefully, and simmer gently 4–5 minutes. Lift out with a perforated spoon, drain for a second, then lay the eggs on top of the puréed peas and dribble a little cream over the top of them. Cut rinds off bacon, chop rashers into strips, and fry in a little butter till crisp. Sprinkle the bacon pieces over the eggs and peas. Add a little more butter to the pan and fry small triangles of bread till golden. Stick round the peas and serve.

If you have two frying pans, or a shallow pan in which to poach the eggs (a roasting pan would do), it would be quicker to prepare the eggs, bacon strips and bread croûtons simultaneously, in the separate pans.

SALMON SOUFFLÉ (*2 helpings*)

1 small tin salmon, ¼ pint white sauce, 4 eggs, paprika, salt, butter

1. Turn out the tinned salmon, keeping the liquid. Pick out any bones and mash it with a fork.
2. Take two mixing bowls, one large, one smaller, and carefully break *three* yolks into the larger bowl and *four* whites into the smaller one. Whisk whites till firm but not too dry.
3. Make white sauce base for soufflé – a soufflé, analytically speaking, is a flavoured white sauce base aerated with beaten egg white. Combine in a pan 1 level dessertspoon flour, 1 oz. butter, ¼ pint milk (roughly ⅔ breakfast cup) and stir over low heat till thick. Add salmon liquid from tin, pinch of salt, 1 tsp. paprika and stir together. Now stir in the mashed salmon, heating till warmed through.
4. Grease a soufflé dish with a little butter. Whisk up egg yolks and stir in sauce/salmon mixture thoroughly. Into this, you now fold the beaten egg whites, using a circular action as if you were turning a sewing machine handle. The idea is to distribute the egg white throughout the heavier salmon base, but not to labour the point to the extent of driving out all the air bubbles.
5. Turn the whole lot into the dish and bake in pre-heated

moderate-to-hot oven (gas 6, 400°F., 205°C.) for 20–25 minutes, until the soufflé is well risen and the top is firm and slightly browned.

Making a soufflé, as I have said before, is not at all difficult as long as you do it methodically, stage by stage. If you deviate from the routine you are apt to get flustered and this will spoil your appetite if not the soufflé.

Tinned tuna fish makes an even more substantial dish. A few peas are all you need with this.

CHINESE SHRIMPS AND PEAS (*2 helpings*)

Chinese dishes like this one are quick to make and very appetizing, so if you have to do a lot of cooking in a hurry it is worth your while to stock up on the extra ingredients needed. Stem ginger is expensive, but one jar lasts a long time. Everything happens at once, in this sort of quick-fry cooking, so it is essential to have all the ingredients ready in separate saucers or bowls, to save confusion.

1 small tin shrimps, 1 medium packet frozen peas, 2 cloves garlic, 1 small piece stem ginger, 2 Tbs. soya sauce, $\frac{1}{2}$ Tbs. cornflour, water, salt, rice

1. Put salted water on to boil for the rice (*see* p. 86). Open tinned shrimps. Put frozen peas in pan with a little water to simmer till thawed.
2. Chop garlic cloves and stem ginger together finely. Mix shrimp liquor, cornflour and 1 Tbs. soya sauce together in a cup.
3. Put rice in to boil, taking a time-check for 12 minutes. Drain peas. Put frying pan over gentle heat to warm up, with 1 Tbs. oil.
4. When rice has a few minutes to go, start frying garlic and ginger gently, stirring to prevent sticking. Add shrimps, still stirring, then well-drained peas and 1 Tbs. soya sauce and a

little (about ½ cup) water. Spoon a little of the juice from the pan into the cornflour mixture, stir and pour the lot into the pan, stirring quickly to distribute it.

5. Drain rice, holding colander under running hot water for a minute to wash off starch. Shake it briefly and return to pan over low heat for a minute or two, covered, to dry off a little.

6. The juice in the frying pan should now be thick and clear. If it seems too thick add a little hot water.

7. Pile the rice into bowls or soup plates, spoon the shrimp mixture on top, and sprinkle a little extra soya sauce over it all if you like the taste. Chopsticks are the correct implements but it tastes just as nice eaten with a spoon.

GRILLED HERRING OR MACKEREL WITH MUSTARD

Have the fish cleaned and opened out flat like a kipper. Smear both sides fairly generously with mustard – English or French. Put a little butter in the grill pan, after removing the grid. When it begins to sizzle, put the fish in, skin side up, and immediately turn it over and continue cooking 5 minutes or so. It will not need to be turned again.

A squeeze of lemon juice heightens the flavour. Plain boiled potatoes are the best accompaniment to highly seasoned fish dishes.

COD STEAKLETS AND AÏOLI*

Frozen cod steaklets, even fish fingers, can be made into quite a presentable meal at short notice if you grill them or fry them in breadcrumbs and serve them with a bowl of garlic mayonnaise, or aïoli (see p. 40).

Thaw the steaklets out a little at room temperature. Rub salt, pepper and a very little mustard well into them. Then you can *either* brush them with melted butter and grill them in the grill pan (minus grid) previously heated with a little butter in the bottom, turning them over as soon as the bottom side has come into contact with the hot butter, *or* brush them with beaten egg, roll them in breadcrumbs and fry them in a little butter and oil till brown all over.

Serve with a few plainly boiled potatoes, green beans and the aïoli.

If you hate garlic, try the Remoulade Sauce recipe on p. 39.

CRAB PILAFF (*4 helpings*)

1 medium tin crab, ¾ lb. Patna rice, 2 large onions, parsley, 1 small packet frozen peas, paprika, salt, pepper, butter, 1 lemon

Throw rice into lots of boiling salted water, and time to cook for 12 minutes. Slice and chop onions fairly finely and fry gently in butter till soft. Put peas in a very little salted water and simmer till cooked. Take crab from tin and remove bony parts. Flake it with a fork. When rice is ready, drain off the water in a colander, run hot water from the tap over it for a minute to wash off starch and return to pan to dry off, covered, on lowest possible heat. When the rice grains seem dry and separated, add the crab, onions and peas, stirring together with a fork. Add paprika, salt and pepper to taste, and a good knob of butter. Cover, and leave over lowest possible heat for a few minutes to allow the crab to heat up, and the flavours to mix. Just before serving add a generous spoonful of finely chopped parsley, and a good squeeze of lemon juice, and fork it all up lightly.

Plain green salad, with French dressing (1 spoon vinegar to 3 olive oil, salt, pepper, sugar and mustard) goes best with this.

Like most pilaff dishes you can add or subtract ingredients. Diced green pepper fried with the onions, could be used instead of peas. Shreds of tinned red pepper and a few shrimps are good too. A couple of Tbs. of grated cheese (preferably Parmesan or a dry pungent cheese) alter the character of the pilaff completely.

The Pauper's Cookbook

Any leftovers make a pleasant salad if you stir in a little French dressing.

FRIED SPRATS* (*2 helpings*)

Sprats are the cheapest fish meal available and very tasty too.

¾ lb. sprats, flour, salt, pepper, 1 lemon

Put a few tablespoons flour, plus a pinch of salt and some pepper, into a paper bag. Wipe the sprats, put them in the bag and shake them around till well coated. Heat some butter or oil – vegetable oil is excellent for frying fish as it is practically tasteless – in a frying pan till smoking hot, then fry the sprats, turning them in one solid mass with a spatula to brown them on both sides.

Eat them just as they are with brown bread and butter and a squeeze of lemon juice.

HASH* (*2 helpings*)

1 small tin corned beef, 2 or 3 leftover boiled potatoes, leftover cabbage or Brussels sprouts, 2 onions, salt, pepper, butter

Chop onions roughly and fry in a little butter till soft. Add diced potatoes, chopped cabbage or sprouts, and fry gently till they are warmed through. Cut up corned beef into chunks and add to the frying pan. Cook over moderate heat, stirring from time to time, until the corned beef has mingled with the other ingredients into a sort of mush. Use a little more butter if the mixture looks dry and in danger of sticking to the pan. Add lots of pepper and a little salt if needed – though corned beef is salty enough, so don't overdo it. You can, if you like, break a couple of eggs on top of the hash, at this point, and cover the pan till they are set.

If you feel the need for extra vegetables, I suggest boiled

carrots. Hash is improved by tomato ketchup or Worcestershire Sauce.

LIVER AU POIVRE (*2–3 helpings*)

Everyone knows steak au poivre, where the raw meat is coated in crushed peppercorns before grilling or frying. Liver au poivre is my own variant and is both very good and very cheap as meat dishes go these days. Use pig's liver, much cheaper than lamb's. The secret of palatable liver is not to overcook it. The quick fry method here, plus the coating of peppercorns, keeps the meat tender and gives it an excellent flavour.

½ lb. pig's liver, 1 rounded dessertspoon black peppercorns, 2 Tbs. cooking oil

With a sharp knife slice the liver into narrow strips about a quarter of an inch thick. Crush peppercorns to a gritty consistency in a Mouli grinder, or mortar, or, failing that, by folding them in a tea towel and banging with a blunt instrument. Sprinkle over sliced liver till well coated. Heat oil in frying pan. Drop in sliced liver and fry quickly, turning with a spoon till lightly browned on all sides. As soon as the liver pieces have stiffened, without being hard, they are done – approximately three minutes. Good with chips and a green salad.

STUFFED GAMMON ROLLS (*4 helpings*)

A handy, economical way with gammon is to buy a good sized boned joint, store it wrapped in the fridge to prevent drying out, and slice thinly for bacon (better flavour than commercial rashers) or thickly for gammon. A sweet stuffing, as here, is good with gammon and makes the slices go further.

4 slices gammon or bacon about ¼ inch thick, 1 oz. fresh white

breadcrumbs, 1 Tbs. melted butter, 1 large Tbs. chopped walnuts (optional), 1 large Tbs. chopped raisins or sultanas, small pinch sage, ½ pint cider, brown sugar, mustard

Mix breadcrumbs, melted butter, sultanas or raisins, nuts, sage and salt and pepper together. Put a spoonful on each slice of gammon, roll up, spear with a toothpick, or tie with a bit of cotton, and lay them in a fireproof dish. Mix ½ pint cider (you could use stock) with a little brown sugar and ½ tsp. mustard, pour over the bacon. Lay a piece of buttered paper over the top and bake in a moderate oven (gas 4, 350°F., 180°C.) for about ¾ hour.

As this is an Irish dish you should dish up steamed buttered potatoes with it. Plain boiled rice would go equally well.

POACHED SAUSAGE AND HOT POTATO SALAD* (2 *helpings*)

A hot potato salad, if you have never tried it, combines very pleasantly with those cheap smoked sausage rings stocked by most supermarkets and delicatessens.

1 smoked sausage, 2 large potatoes, 1 tsp. dry mustard or rather more French mustard, salt, black pepper, 1 Tbs. finely chopped onion, a little chopped parsley (optional), 4 Tbs. oily vinaigrette dressing

Put on two pans of water. When it boils, put scrubbed, unpeeled potatoes in one pan and the sausage ring in the other. The sausage should simmer, not boil. I think the flavour is improved by removing the polythene wrap, never mind what the makers tell you.

After 20 minutes or so, prod the potatoes with a fork. When they are tender, take them out and peel them, holding them in a cloth. Cut them into smallish chunks. Stir the mustard into the vinaigrette dressing and pour over the potatoes, spooning them about gently to spread the dressing evenly. Sprinkle with salt and black pepper. Add the chopped onion and parsley, and spoon around a bit more.

Take the sausage out of its pan, cut it into chunks and serve with a few pickled gherkins or onions, which go well with this dish, and the salad.

For a change you could try Eliza Acton's Potato Salad, an excellent invention of this pioneer Victorian cookery writer. For this the potatoes are mashed. You also need 2 hard-boiled eggs, and a dash of anchovy essence if available.

Separate egg yolks from whites. Mash yolks and stir into the mustardy vinaigrette dressing, together with salt, pepper and a dash of anchovy essence. Chop whites roughly. Mash the potatoes, stir in the dressing, the chopped onion and egg whites. You can dispense with the parsley here.

In the north they make the latter salad with bottled salad cream with excellent results.

KIDNEYS EN CHEMISE (*2 helpings*)

2 sheep's kidneys, 2 round bread rolls, butter, salt, pepper, dash of Worcestershire Sauce

Cut the tops off 2 rolls, remove some of the crumbs and butter thickly. Sprinkle on salt and pepper. Skin and core the kidneys and put them inside the rolls, with a dash of Worcestershire Sauce. Replace the bread lids on top and bake the rolls in a medium oven for 20–30 minutes. When cooked they will have absorbed most of the juice from the kidneys.

SLICED TONGUE IN CAPER SAUCE (*2 helpings*)

1 small tin tongue, 1 Tbs. capers, $\frac{1}{4}$–$\frac{1}{2}$ pint stock (hot water plus bouillon cube), $\frac{1}{2}$ Tbs. cornflour, dash of soya or Worcestershire Sauce

Slice up the tongue. Any jelly with it goes into the sauce.

Mix the stock with the cornflour and heat in a pan till it thickens. Add a dash of soya or Worcestershire Sauce, more for colour than flavour, and stir in the capers.

Pour this over the tongue slices in a shallow oven dish and bake for ½ hour in a moderate oven (gas 4, 350°F., 180°C.).

Serve with plain boiled rice, with plenty of butter stirred into it, and boiled carrots finished off with butter and a little sugar.

A MEAL IN A POTATO*

Large baked potatoes with something tucked inside are a god-send when you are hard up. You need 1 or 2 large potatoes per person, some grated cheese, butter, salt and pepper. If you want to make a more solid meal of it, add 1 egg to each potato.

Scrub the potatoes, dry, and rub salt into the skins. Bake in a hot oven (gas 7, 425°F., 220°C.) till they feel soft when pinched – about an hour. Cut a cap off each potato. Scoop out a little pulp. Put a nut of butter and a handful of grated cheese into the hollow. Add pepper and salt. Return to the oven for a few minutes. If you want eggs too, scoop out rather more of the potato pulp, proceed as before except that you break an egg in before putting back the cap. Cook 7 minutes or till egg is set.

A substantial version of this dish is to have kidneys in the potatoes.

Scrub and bake potatoes for 1 hour as above. Cut a slice off the top and scoop out some of the inside. Skin the kidneys and rub in salt, pepper and a little mustard. Roll each kidney in a rasher of bacon, put in a potato case. Wrap the potatoes in foil with a scrap of butter and bake for 1 hour longer. The kidney gravy is soaked up by the potato.

Leftover baked potatoes are tasty fried up, skins and all, as a rough-and-ready version of pommes sautées. Chop roughly, and fry in hot oil or dripping.

POTATO LATKES* (*4–6 helpings*)

This is a Jewish dish, and a very tasty one, substantial enough to serve on its own with some slices of garlic sausage and a plate of pickled gherkins. Latkes, definitely not recommended for calorie counters, are made of grated raw potato and onion, bound with egg and flour, and fried till brown on both sides.

1 lb. grated raw potato, 1 Tbs. grated or finely chopped onion, 2 large eggs, 2 Tbs. flour, salt and black pepper

Peel and grate the potatoes into a mixing bowl. Add the onion and flour, then stir in the well-beaten eggs, salt and pepper. The mixture should be soft enough to drop from a spoon. If it seems too dry or stiff, add another egg. Heat some oil in a frying pan and, when it is hot, drop in spoonfuls of the mixture and fry till brown on both sides, turning the potato cakes with a spatula. Serve at once.

POTATO, APPLE AND CAPER SALAD (*4 helpings*)

4 potatoes boiled in their skins, 2 small eating apples, 1 level Tbs. capers, vinaigrette (*see* p. 37), squeeze of lemon juice, salt and pepper

Peel potatoes and leave to cool. Core and peel the apples. Slice both thinly and combine with capers and dressing. Squeeze lemon juice over and season with salt and pepper to taste.

This is good with most cold meat, particularly ham.

CARAMEL ORANGES

This is a simple fruit salad of sliced oranges glorified by a sprinkling of crushed caramel, like amber chips. Use a sharp knife to prepare the oranges and take off every scrap of outer pith, which sticks in one's teeth and spoils the taste. Hold the oranges over the dish you are serving them in while preparing them so none of the juice is wasted.

Allow 1½ oranges per person, or more if you can afford them.

Slice the peel off the oranges, downwards rather than round and round. Trim off every bit of pith. Slice oranges thickly, pick out the pips. Make a little liquid to go over them either by squeezing the juice of 1 extra orange and sweetening it with a little sugar, or, if you have time, boiling up a little sugar, water and orange juice and pouring it on when cooled.

To make the caramel, heat 3 Tbs. sugar in an enamelled pan with a little water, till it melts and goes brown – golden brown, not treacle coloured. Pour on to a sheet of greased paper to cool. When it is hard and brittle shatter by hitting it with a heavy bottle or something. Scatter the fragments over your salad.

Whipped cream can be served along with this but I don't think it is necessary.

BANANA SOUFFLÉ★ (2–3 helpings)

Mash 3 large ripe bananas. Stir in 2–3 Tbs. sugar and 1 Tbs. lemon juice. Butter your soufflé dish and stand a pan of hot water for it in your oven, which should be pre-heated (gas 6, 400°F., 204°C.). Beat up 3 egg whites stiff, but not so dry they crumble. Blend in a pinch of baking powder and fold the whites into the banana pulp.

Turn the soufflé mixture into the dish, stand the dish in the pan of hot water in the oven and bake for ½ hour, or until well risen and firm on top.

BAKED, BUTTERED APRICOTS★ (4 helpings)

A remarkably nice and simply made pudding.

1 small tin apricot halves, 4 thick slices of bread, butter, sugar, cinnamon

Drain the apricots, reserving the syrup. Cut the crusts off the bread. Fresh white bread is best for this dish. Butter thickly on both sides. Lay the slices over the bottom of a baking tin.

Press the apricot halves firmly into the buttered bread. Sprinkle sugar (preferably Demerara) generously over the top, and a dusting of cinnamon. Bake in a moderate oven (gas 4, 350°F., 180°C.) till the bread is crisp and golden (about ½ hour).

You can serve these with a sauce made from the apricot syrup thickened with a little cornflour, or with plain cream.

Fresh apricots, plums or peaches are even better done this way.

BAKED BANANAS*

I think this is the nicest way of eating bananas. It is also very quick and easy to prepare.

Allow 2 large bananas per person. Slice the bananas in half lengthwise and arrange them in a flat fireproof dish. Sprinkle with 1 Tbs. brown sugar, or more, if you are using a lot of bananas. Squeeze the juice of 1 orange and ½ lemon over the lot. Sprinkle with a little grated orange and lemon peel. Dot fairly liberally with butter and bake, uncovered, in a moderate oven (gas 4, 350°F., 180°C.), until the bananas are soft and the other ingredients have turned to a thin syrup (about 20 minutes).

Serve exactly as they are – cream would be too cloying. A few sultanas sprinkled over the dish is a pleasant addition. And, if you have any rum around the place, a spoonful added with the other ingredients gives you Baked Bananas Creole.

SOUFFLÉ OMELETTE* (*2 helpings*)

A nice quick pudding, which you can fill with whatever is available – apricot jam, apple purée, even marmalade.

3 eggs, 2 Tbs. thick cream (optional), 1 Tbs. caster sugar, 2 oz. butter

Beat the yolks, cream and sugar together till smooth. Whip up the whites stiffly and fold lightly into the yolks. Melt the butter in a frying pan over a moderate flame, pour in the egg mixture, level it off with a spoon and leave till small bubbles appear on the top. Then spoon in the jam or whatever filling you are using, fold the omelette over and sprinkle the top with sugar.

Serve at once.

TOASTED CHEESE AND ONION SANDWICHES

Bread, butter, Cheddar cheese, 1 onion

You need a bit less than $\frac{1}{4}$ lb. Cheddar for 2 sandwiches. Toast bread on one side only. Butter the other side, pile with grated cheese and grill until the cheese melts. Add a few thin slices of raw onion and clap the slices together. If you don't fancy raw onion, sliced tomatoes are just as good.

CHASSE (*2 helpings*)

I am including this recipe, originally a country-house breakfast dish, because it is an excellent way of combining the sort of odds and ends you can usually scrape together in the most depleted larder into a comforting little meal. The quantities I have given can be varied according to what is available – tinned tomatoes can be used, instead of fresh, or even a generous tablespoonful of tomato purée, at a pinch.

1 onion, 5 tomatoes, 3 cooked potatoes, a slice of ham or 2–3 rashers of bacon, 2–3 oz. grated cheese, paprika, dash of Worcestershire Sauce, 2 poached eggs, nut of butter, salt

Fry the onion lightly in the butter, then add chopped, skinned tomatoes and chopped ham or bacon. When these are hot add diced potatoes and a little water and cook slowly for

5 minutes. Just before serving add a dash of Worcestershire Sauce and stir in the grated cheese mixed with a good pinch of paprika. Serve with a poached egg on each helping.

QUICK WELSH RAREBIT* (*2 helpings*)

When you are in a tearing hurry, or faced with the job of concocting a meal out of a lump of stale cheese and some dry bread, Welsh Rarebit seems the obvious answer. The best cheese for this, I think, is Caerphilly, which gives a sharper, lighter texture than Cheddar, but I realize that this is a counsel of perfection.

$\frac{1}{4}-\frac{1}{2}$ lb. cheese, 2 slices of bread, 1 tsp. dry mustard, dash of Worcestershire Sauce, salt, pepper, butter, 1 egg

Grate the cheese, mix in the dry mustard, salt, pepper and Worcestershire Sauce, and bind with the beaten egg. If you can spare it, a knob of butter worked in helps. Toast the bread on one side only. Spread the other side thickly with the mixture and stick it under the grill till the cheese is puffy and lightly browned. Eat at once.

Should you not have so much as an egg, you can thicken your cheese mixture (and make it go a bit further too) by stirring in a little cornflour, or flour, mixed with a little milk or water or beer. In that case you should really cook the Rarebit in a saucepan for a few minutes to give the flour a chance to thicken. Then brown under the grill.

A couple of poached eggs on top, should you be well supplied with eggs, turns this into a Buck Rarebit.

Programmed Eating

The practical advantages of planning, buying and cooking the next week's meals at one fell swoop are so obvious I won't dwell on them, except to mention that a seven-day plan like this saves money as well as time, because it cuts down wastage. The essence of the scheme is that every scrap gets used, bones, skin, even the cooking water. No little saucers growing fur in dark corners.

This chapter is not intended for experienced housewives, who will have evolved their own system over the years, but for beginners at the game, especially young working wives, who want to do other things with their free time besides shop and cook. I know from experience how perplexing it can be to be set adrift on a sea of recipes with a limited sum to spend and a week's meals to cater for. You spend hours choosing likely recipes, hours more working out just how much of everything you need. At the last minute, you lose your nerve and double all the quantities. Half of it goes bad, or sour, or soft, and you end up sneaking out for a packet of sausages. It's one way to learn, of course, but an expensive one.

First, a few words about general strategy. (This plan only allows for one main meal a day, incidentally. Breakfasts most people can cope with anyway, and a working couple presumably lunch out.) On Friday evening you choose your menu and make out a list, on Saturday morning you have a marathon shopping expedition and on Saturday afternoon, when you have got your breath back, you tackle the cooking. Something like that.

Build your week's meals round one big, relatively costly item – a boiling chicken, bacon joint, casserole, meat loaf. All these, as you will see, give you at least three meals plus odd perks, in some cases, like soup. Make one or two dishes which will keep at the same time as you are preparing the big dish – a pâté, for instance, a large milk pudding and a fruit compote to eat with it. If you have any energy left cook a couple of flan cases 'blind', to be stored in an airtight tin and filled with different mixtures later in the week. Alternatively you can make the pastry the day you eat it. By judiciously interweaving pâté meals and flan meals you can make it round to day one again, without complaints about having to eat the same thing day in, day out. What is more, the outlay involved will be modest and the daily stint in the kitchen numbered in minutes not hours.

For economy's sake I suggest buying boiling chicken and bacon because that way you get the stock too, which is useful for soups and sauces. A good boiling chicken is cheaper than a roasting bird, and has a lot of meat on it. Don't buy exotic meats as your main item – venison, for instance – because, although it may cost less to start with, one rapidly tires of anything with a very pronounced flavour.

The outline I have given above does not include trimmings – fresh vegetables, fruit, salads. Suggestions for these are given with the specimen menus. Vary them according to what is in season and cheap. As a general rule, though, eat up the perishable stuff (soft fruit) straight away, or cook it, and lay in a good stock of carrots, potatoes, onions, lemons, sprouts, etc., which keep well. Lettuces, parsley, curly endive should be washed, shaken almost dry and stored in polythene bags. They will keep up to a week like this, in a cool place. You will also need the odd tin of tomato purée, packet of spaghetti, rice, cheese, eggs plus the usual herbs and spices. A quick glance at the recipes with the menus will show you in more detail.

I am giving four weekly menus in detail, with ideas for a few others based on recipes elsewhere in this book.

Menu 1

This menu features chicken, liver pâté, Alsatian onion tart. Also chicken noodle soup. For puddings: junket, fresh fruit, chocolate mousse, fruit compote.

Shopping

Get a medium-sized boiling fowl, not a frozen chicken, as these have less meat and flavour. Go to a good butcher. Ask him to throw the chicken feet in with the giblets; these improve the stock. At the same time ask him to mince 1 lb. pig's liver together with ¾ lb. pork belly for the pâté. You also need ¼ lb. back fat in one large sheet, or ¼ lb. fat bacon, to line the pâté dish with.

In the vegetable line buy enough salad to go with three cold meals – 2 lettuces, or 1 big lettuce and 1 lb. of tomatoes, or the equivalent of what is in season. Also 2–3 lb. potatoes, some parsley, 1 lb. sprouts, 1 lb. carrots, 3 lb. onions. Stock up on garlic. Buy some fresh fruit in season, a few oranges, apples, or soft fruit. Also some fruit for stewing in a compote. (This could be dried fruit in winter, especially at the beginning of the year, when it is cheaper.)

In the way of stores you will need the usual eggs, butter, milk, bread, plus 1 lb. rice, 1 packet spaghetti, Cheddar or Parmesan for cheese sauce. Also salad dressing ingredients, flour, curry paste, tomato purée or 1 small tin peeled tomatoes, rennet, mustard, Worcestershire Sauce, chocolate.

Preparation and Cooking

First mix the pâté ingredients together (*see* p. 145), and leave to stand while you put the chicken on. Put the chicken into a large saucepan with giblets, feet, vegetables – 1 onion with a clove stuck in it, a sliced carrot or two – and a bayleaf or a sprig of parsley and thyme. Add cold water just to cover, a little salt and pepper. Put a lid on the pan and bring it to the boil. Then lower heat to simmering point (or transfer to the oven), and cook gently for $1\frac{1}{2}$–2 hours.

While the chicken is cooking, make the junket and Chocolate Mousse (enough for four helpings), both easy puddings. (*See* pp. 143 and 192.) Make the fruit compote. Either put the fruit, with water to cover and sugar, in the oven (low shelf) and leave it till tender, while the pâté is cooking above, or make a sugar-and-water syrup separately (*see* Gooseberry Compote p. 82), and simmer the fruit in it till cooked.

Put all the puddings away in a cool place.

Line the pâté dish, put in the mixture and cook as directed. If you have any spare energy, now is the time to make the pastry for the Alsatian Onion Tart. It can rest while the pâté is cooking and bake while you are finishing the dinner preparations. Wash the salad materials and store them in bags. Look at the chicken to see how it is getting on. Half an hour before the meal put water on for rice and vegetables and make the sauce for the chicken.

Day1: Meal consists of slices of chicken breast on rice, with a Vinaigrette Sauce (recipe on p. 37), and buttered carrots. Fresh fruit to follow.

Check to see whether the pâté is cooked – it should start coming away from the sides of the dish. If it is, move from oven, turn up the heat and roll out the pastry, line the flan case and bake as directed (*see* p. 101). The fruit can go on cooking in the oven, low down. Put the rice and carrots on to cook. Store the pâté away. Turn the heat off under the chicken and leave it in the stock. When the vegetables are done, slice some of the breast off thinly, lay it on the rice and serve.

The pastry should be done by the time you have finished your meal. Leave it to cool, on a rack if possible, before storing in an airtight tin. The chicken can be left to cool in the stock, which helps prevent it drying out. Lift it out and drain when cool, and put it on a plate or in a covered bowl.

The following are meal suggestions for the rest of the week. A good-sized bird ought to provide one bits-and-pieces meal, as well as three substantial ones. Remember to boil the chicken stock up for 10 minutes, covered, once a day, to kill off bacteria.

Day 2: Sliced breast heated up in cheese sauce, made as for Eggs in Cheese Sauce (*see* p. 122), eaten with spaghetti or noodles and buttered sprouts. Make the sauce first, lay the chicken slices in it and heat slowly in the oven for about $\frac{1}{2}$ hour. In hot weather, a good alternative would be the same meat eaten cold coated with a well-seasoned mayonnaise. Fresh fruit, or compote and junket to follow.

Day 3: Chicken Noodle Soup made from some of the stock, strained, with a handful of noodles boiled up in it. Devilled drumsticks to follow, with baked potatoes and salad. Cheese for afters.

Day 4: A break from chicken is indicated. But pick scraps off the carcase and decide how you will cook them for the next day. A curry, or added to savoury rice. Alternatively, you can put them into a small bowl with some of the strained stock and eat as Chicken in Aspic with salad. This day's menu is pâté, boiled or baked potatoes, salad. Chocolate Mousse to follow.

Day 5: French Onion Soup to start (*see* p. 32) made with the stock. This is very filling. Either curry (*see* recipe which follows) or Chicken in Aspic. Fruit, fresh or compote.

Day 6: Alsatian Onion Tart (*see* p. 103) with tomato salad. Chocolate Mousse to follow.

Day 7: Pâté with baked potatoes and salad. Any leftovers in the pudding line. Or, if you are thoroughly sick of them all, try a Soufflé Omelette (*see* p. 135) with a jam filling, which only takes a few minutes to make.

SAUCE FOR CHICKEN SLICES

Make a well-seasoned Vinaigrette Sauce (*see* p. 37), with finely chopped parsley and onion added to it. Just before serving, mix in the yolks of 2 soft-boiled eggs and the chopped whites. This is a French sauce for boiled chicken, and surprisingly good.

JUNKET AND CREAM*

Junket is such a simple, unpretentious pudding that it tends to be overlooked. Personally, I much prefer it to the current favourite, yoghourt, especially with a little thick cream. Dressed up with Banana Purée (*see* below) it is quite nice enough to produce at a dinner party.

1 pint gold-topped milk, 1 dessertspoon sugar, 1 small tsp. rennet, $\frac{1}{4}$ pint double cream, nutmeg or cinnamon

Heat milk till just tepid over low flame. Add sugar (according to taste), stir well, pour into a flat dish, stir in the rennet and leave to set. Sprinkle with a little cinnamon or grated nutmeg before serving.

For a slightly more elaborate version, mash 2 ripe bananas till very soft and frothy, adding a little sugar. Put them in the bottom of the flat dish, pour the junket over and leave to set as before.

DEVILLED CHICKEN LEGS (2 *helpings*)

2 cooked chicken legs, mustard, Worcestershire Sauce, dry breadcrumbs, 1 oz. butter, salt, pepper

Remove skin from legs. Make a little thick mustard, using Worcestershire Sauce instead of water, and coat the legs with this, rubbing it well in, together with a little salt and pepper. Roll the legs in breadcrumbs till well coated. Pre-heat the grill. Melt a little butter in the grill pan (removing wire grid) or use a fireproof dish. Dab a few little bits of butter on the legs and grill on both sides for 5–6 minutes, or longer if the legs are particularly large.

This is a useful recipe, too, for raw chicken legs, especially the frozen kind, which tend to be rather tasteless. The procedure with uncooked chicken (well thawed, if frozen) is the same except that they will need cooking roughly twice as long, turning frequently, under a not too hot grill.

Serve these devilled legs just as they are with the juices from the pan poured over them, and a watercress salad. Or with boiled rice and mustard sauce if you want to make more of a meal of them.

MUSTARD SAUCE

1 small onion, 1 tsp. mustard, butter, $\frac{1}{2}$ Tbs. flour, $\frac{1}{2}$ pint stock or $\frac{1}{2}$ pint boiling water and $\frac{1}{2}$ bouillon cube

Chop onion finely and fry in a little butter till soft. Stir in flour and mustard, add stock and cook till it thickens. Add salt and pepper to taste.

CURRIED CHICKEN* (*2 helpings*)

This is really a thick ragoût of onion, tomato and herbs, strongly seasoned with curry paste, in which the bits of cooked chicken are heated up. Purists probably would not recognize it as curry, but it is a tasty dish and nice and quick to make. Serve it with boiled rice, chutney and a garnish of thinly sliced banana.

Cooked chicken pieces, 2 onions, 1 small tin peeled tomatoes, bayleaf, 1 clove garlic, pinch thyme, curry paste ($\frac{1}{2}$ Tbs. gives a fairly hot curry), a few sultanas or raisins, salt, pepper, pinch sugar, oil or butter

Heat a little oil or butter in a frying pan. Add chopped onions and garlic and fry over moderate heat till soft. Add curry paste and stir for a minute or two. Put in the peeled tomatoes, herbs, seasoning, dried fruit and pinch sugar. Reduce heat and simmer till the sauce has thickened and some of the tomato liquid has evaporated. Now add the cooked chicken, cut into roughly equal pieces. Heat through gently but do not allow to boil. Stir and taste. Add more curry paste if liked. (I generally use vindaloo paste which has more flavour than the usual curry paste, but it is very hot, so should be used cautiously.)

Raw chicken, fish and meat can be curried in much the same way, except that the curry paste should be well rubbed into the pieces before cooking, and they will of course need to be fried and then simmered as long as is needed to cook them. Other suitable vegetables can be added – diced green pepper, tinned red pepper, okra, courgettes, celery, small pieces of cauliflower. Instead of tomatoes you could use stock, either on its own or flavoured with coconut milk for a subtle, mild curry flavour.

LIVER PÂTÉ

1 lb. pig's liver, $\frac{3}{4}$ lb. belly of pork, $\frac{1}{4}$ lb. back fat or fat bacon,

2 cloves garlic, 8 juniper berries, 6 peppercorns, large pinch salt, 2 bayleaves

If you give the butcher a little notice he will usually mince the liver and belly of pork up together for you. If you have to do it yourself, plunging the liver into boiling water for a couple of minutes makes the job easier and less messy. Put the meat through the mincer twice for smooth results. Chop half the back fat or bacon into small cubes. Chop garlic finely, bruise peppercorns and juniper berries by bashing them in a bowl with a wooden spoon. Mix together all ingredients except bayleaves and leave to stand for 1–2 hours so that the flavours mingle. Then pack the pâté ingredients into a small earthenware casserole, lay the 2 bayleaves on top, and cover with a lattice of strips cut from the remaining bacon. Cook, uncovered, standing in a roasting pan with 1 inch or so of water in it (gas 2, 300°F., 150°C.) for approximately 1½ hours or until the pâté begins to come away from the sides of the casserole. Lay a piece of greaseproof paper on top, then a small saucer or plate, and press this with a couple of kitchen weights, or a full jam jar. When cold, remove weights and paper. If you are not going to eat the pâté straight away, pour a little melted lard over the top to seal it, and store in a cool place. Storing in the fridge tends to dry a pâté out.

Menu 2

This weekly menu centres on a cut of gammon or boiling bacon, Haricot Bean Soup, Jellied Tongue. For puddings: Cheesecake, Baked Apricots, fresh fruit.

I suggest gammon rather than a more conventional roast because it is nicer cold (unless you can afford good beef), the stock makes good bean soup and the leftovers are versatile. Tongue is cheap, fairly simple to prepare, can be used to eke out the bacon and cán also be eaten hot, and cold, on its own. This would be a two-day cooking operation because the Bean Soup must be made a day or so after the gammon is cooked.

Shopping

Buy a piece of gammon, with or without a bone, weighing 3 lb. or slightly more. Also a tongue (*see* recipe p. 149).

In the vegetable line you need 3–4 lb. potatoes, vegetables for two hot meals – carrots, sprouts, beans, spinach. Also salad materials for three meals – in winter, a coleslaw would be a good choice (*see* p. 74). This requires a small cabbage, celery or grated apple, carrots, 1 lettuce. Also some fresh fruit.

Dry stores should include 1 lb. haricot beans, 1 lb. dried or tinned apricots (large tin), Patna rice, $\frac{1}{4}$ lb. cream cheese for Cheesecake and a few sultanas. Check that you have capers, mustard, gelatine, cloves, brown sugar, flour.

Buy rather more eggs than usual because you will need them for the flan and poached eggs later.

Preparation and Cooking

Soak gammon in cold water the minute you get home. Also apricots, if dried. Also haricot beans. If you are short of pans cook the tongue in the afternoon (*see* p. 149) before the gammon, which should be started 2–2$\frac{1}{2}$ hours before you want to eat it. Make the pastry for 2 flans and leave to rest for a couple of hours. Turn the tongue into a bowl with stock and gelatine to set. Put the gammon on to cook (*see* p. 183).

Make Cheesecake filling and bake in one pastry case, with apricots (if dried) in sugared water on lower shelf, as for a compote. When Cheesecake is done put in the other flan case and bake blind. Store in an airtight tin. Take out the apricots. Bake the gammon as directed (*keeping* the cooking water) with a few of the apricots round it in the tin, and some baked potatoes squeezed round on the top shelf. (These ought perhaps to go in earlier on, during one of the previous baking operations.) Prepare and cook vegetables to eat with gammon.

Suggested menus for the week

Day 1: Hot Baked Gammon with apricots, baked potatoes and one vegetable. Fresh fruit or cheese to follow.

Day 2: Cold gammon and tongue with mustard, baked or boiled potatoes, coleslaw or salad. Cheesecake. (Make the Bean Soup as directed, *see* p. 33.)

Day 3: The same again, if there seems to be plenty of gammon. (You need a small cupful of pieces for an Egg and Bacon Flan, p. 45.) Baked Apricots on Bread (*see* p. 134).

Day 4: Bean Soup. Tongue slices in Caper Sauce (*see* p. 131) with rice and vegetable. Cheesecake or fresh fruit.

Day 5: Egg and Bacon Flan with salad. Baked potatoes if you are hungry. Fresh fruit.

Day 6: Remains of Bean Soup, liquid reduced by boiling, sieved to a thick purée, seasoned well, with poached eggs on top. Remaining apricots.

Day 7: Remains of Egg and Bacon Flan to start. Sliced tongue and lettuce. Any leftovers in the pudding line, or cheese to finish.

If you have too little gammon left for two cold meals (this depends on your appetites and the size of the joint), you should be able to get two scrap meals from it – Bacon and Noodle Pie (*see* p. 94), fritters, stuffed onions are possibilities. Or Onion-Bacon-Potato Pie (*see* p. 58), if you are feeling energetic.

I have given a recipe (p. 158) for Garbure, a French peasant soup, which could be made with the bacon stock as an alternative to bean soup, incorporating any odd scraps of meat and the bone, if any.

TONGUE*

A small tongue is a good buy. It will give you one hot and two cold meals for very little trouble on your part. Tongues are sold either salted or fresh. If you buy one fresh, it is a good idea to soak it in some salted water for 1–2 hours before cooking.

In either case, to cook, put it in a pan with water to cover and an assortment of sliced vegetables and herbs – onion, carrot, celery, peppercorns, thyme, parsley, garlic. Bring to the boil slowly, skimming if necessary, cover the pan, and simmer very gently till the tongue is quite tender. This point has been reached when the little bones at the root have almost detached themselves. Leave to cool for a while before taking it out of the liquid. It should now be carefully skinned, and the root part cut off. Eat a few slices hot with some of the cooking liquor, to which you have added a few capers and raisins, reduced to make a sauce.

The remainder should be packed down into a bowl or curled round in a circular dish or tin. Reduce enough of the cooking stock to cover the tongue, by boiling it hard, strain it, add a little powdered gelatine – the proportions are 1 oz. to 1 pint of liquid – and pour over the tongue. Leave in a cool place to set.

CHEESECAKE (4–6 *helpings*)

Cheesecake is quite simple to make and inexpensive compared with the ready-made sort on sale in most delicatessens.

½ lb. cream cheese, ¼ lb. butter, 1 Tbs. sultanas, 4 eggs, vanilla essence, 1 Tbs. sugar

Beat the butter to a soft cream. Work in the cheese, crumbled small, then the sugar, preferably caster sugar, and lastly the well-beaten egg yolks. Whip the whites stiff and fold into the mixture. Sprinkle in the sultanas and a little vanilla essence.

Line a cake tin with short crust pastry and fill with the cheese mixture. Brush the top with a little egg yolk to give it a good colour and bake in a moderate oven (gas 5, 375°F., 190°C.) for approximately 1 hour or until the pastry is golden and the filling firm.

Leave to cool before eating.

Menu 3

Meat Loaf, Irish Stew (Casseroled Lamb Cutlets), smoked sausage and hot potato salad. Puddings: Lemon Meringue Pie, Caramel Custard, fresh fruit.

Shopping

Minced beef, pork and ¼ lb. bacon for the Meat Loaf. Enough lamb cutlets (scrag end) for four helpings, or two meals.

Vegetables: 3–4 lb. potatoes, 2 lb. onions, 1 lb. carrots, garlic. Vegetables in season to accompany four hot meals. Lemons for pie, fresh fruit. Salads for two meals. Parsley.

Groceries: Smoked sausage ring, 1 large tin peeled tomatoes, barley, evaporated milk for custard. Check that you have flour, tomato purée, Worcestershire Sauce, spaghetti, rice. You will also need plenty of eggs for the lemon pie and custard, and cheese.

Preparation and cooking

Mix Meat Loaf ingredients and leave to stand for 1 hour. Make the pastry for lemon pie, and leave to rest. Prepare Irish Stew (*see* p. 62) and bake for three-quarters of specified time. Now get the Meat Loaf ready for baking, also the Lemon Meringue

Pie and Caramel Custard. Put them all in the oven together (the lamb has been put to cool somewhere else), with the Lemon Meringue Pie on top and Meat Loaf and custard side by side. This saves fuel. If you are nervous of the Meat Loaf flavouring the custard put a piece of foil over the top. Time them all separately of course. Half an hour before dining, put on water for rice to eat with the Meat Loaf, make some Tomato Sauce (*see* p. 41) and prepare a vegetable.

Suggested menus for the week

Day 1: Hot Meat Loaf with tomato sauce and rice. Lemon Meringue Pie. Wrap leftover Meat Loaf in foil to stop it drying out.

Day 2: Irish Stew with boiled potatoes and green vegetable. Before re-heating the stew, skim off the fat. Heat in moderate oven for 30–40 minutes. Fresh fruit to follow.

Day 3: Irish Stew in disguise. Add some tomato purée and a little garlic and curry paste to the broth before heating, and serve with rice and a vegetable. Lemon Meringue to follow.

Day 4: Meat Loaf cold, with baked potatoes and salad. Serve it with lots of mustard and a few pickled gherkins if possible. Caramel Custard.

Day 5: Leftovers of Meat Loaf go into baked Spaghetti au Gratin, which is spaghetti boiled till just tender, drained, mixed with a tomato sauce thickened with the meat and covered with a thick layer of grated cheese. Bake 20 minutes in moderate oven. Serve with buttered vegetable. Fresh fruit.

Day 6: Boiled smoked sausage and Hot Potato Salad (*see* p. 130). Green salad. Caramel Custard.

Day 7: Either eggs in cheese sauce with a medley of remaining vegetables, followed by any pudding leftovers or fresh fruit. *Or*

Spanish Omelette incorporating vegetable, bacon, potatoes. (*See* p. 122 for both recipes.)

FAMILY MEAT LOAF (*4–6 helpings, with leftovers*)

An endlessly useful dish which can be eaten hot, or cold. The leftovers can be quickly transformed into stuffed cabbage, to relieve the tedium of eating the same thing several days running.

1 lb. beef mince, $\frac{1}{2}$ lb. minced pork, 2 finely chopped Spanish onions, 2 finely chopped garlic cloves, 2 Tbs. chopped parsley, 2 thick slices stale white bread, stock or tomato purée, 1 Tbs. soya sauce, dash of Worcestershire Sauce, 1 egg, salt, pepper, $\frac{1}{4}$ lb. streaky bacon (optional)

Cut 2 slices stale white bread. Remove crusts, and soak in enough stock or tomato purée plus soya and Worcestershire Sauce to moisten thoroughly, without drenching the bread. Mix the bread with the mince, chopped onion, garlic and parsley. Add a pinch of salt, plenty of pepper, and stir in 1 well-beaten egg to bind. If the meat is on the dry side, without much fat content, add 2 Tbs. melted butter.

To cook, either pack the meat into a loaf tin lined with the bacon, rinds removed, and bake in a moderate oven (gas 4, 350°F., 180°C.) for $1\frac{1}{2}$–2 hours, or until the loaf starts to come away from the sides of the tin. Or shape the meat into a loaf, wrap it in foil, sealing the edges, and bake in an ordinary roasting pan for about the same length of time, uncovering the loaf for the last 20 minutes or so to brown it. This method uses no bacon.

CARAMEL CUSTARD (*4 helpings*)

Caramel custard is hard to beat at any time, but made with evaporated milk it is quite luscious.

1 pint evaporated milk (if the tins don't yield precisely the right

amount make it up with water), 4 eggs, 3 Tbs. sugar, ½ tsp. vanilla essence, 2 Tbs. sugar, water for caramel

First caramelize your pudding mould, which can be a mixing bowl, in which case remember to warm it before putting in the caramel or it may crack.

Melt 2 Tbs. sugar over a very low heat, and then add 1–2 tsp. cold water. Pour the caramel quickly into your mould and twist it around and around to spread the caramel over as much of the surface as possible. Heat the evaporated milk with the 3 Tbs. sugar, stirring till the sugar has melted. Set aside to cool. Beat up the eggs till frothy and stir into the milk. Add ½ tsp. vanilla essence. (Or better still make the custard with vanilla sugar.) Pour the custard into the mould and set the mould in a pan of hot water reaching about half the height of the mould. Cook in pre-heated oven (gas 4, 350°F., 180°C.) for 40 minutes.

The custard is cooked when a knife stuck into it comes out clean. Remove it and leave it to cool before turning out.

Menu 4

This weekly menu features a rich Beef Casserole, braised sausages, tongue. Puddings: fresh fruit, Fig Compote, Caramel Rice.

Shopping

1½–2 lb. shin of beef for the casserole, ½ lb. sausages, 1 tongue.

Vegetables: You need the following for the casserole: onions, carrots, celery, garlic, parsley. Also salad to accompany three meals. Two lb. potatoes. Fresh fruit.

Groceries: ¼ lb. bacon, ¼ lb. black olives, 1 lb. haricot beans, spaghetti, pudding rice, dried figs and muscatels. Check that you have gelatine for the tongue, and plenty of herbs.

You also need 1 big tin peeled tomatoes, or 1 medium and 1 small.

Cooking and preparation

Get the stew in the oven in plenty of time (*see* recipe on p. 155) because shin of beef needs long, slow cooking. Put the tongue on to cook according to the recipe on p. 149. Set haricot beans and figs and muscatels to soak separately. Make custard for Caramel Rice and put the rice into milk to simmer (*see* p. 156). Get caramelized mould ready. Prepare rice as directed and put the pudding into the oven to bake, with the casserole. At this point, add stoned olives to the stew. Skin and prepare tongue as directed, and leave to cool in jelly. Put on water for pasta to eat with casserole. Make sure you do not forget the pudding, which should be left aside to cool. Put the sausages in a cool place, preferably bottom of the fridge.

Suggested meals

Day 1: Beef Casserole Niçoise with pasta. Fresh fruit to follow.

Day 2: Casserole again, but with boiled haricot beans mixed with a little chopped garlic, parsley and butter. Salad, cheese to follow. Keep leftover beans and stew in cool place.

Day 3: Sausages braised in the oven with some of the liquid from the stew and a little tomato purée/cider/stock added, plus some finely chopped onion, and a sprinkling of parsley. (There should still be some of the casserole left.) Cook sausages in moderate oven (gas 4, 350° F., 180° C.) for 45 minutes, or until browned, turning them from time to time. Serve with remaining haricot beans sieved into a purée, adding lots of butter. Fig Compote to follow.

Day 4: Baked Spaghetti (*see* Meat Loaf menu, p. 152, for directions) with remains of casserole spread on top and covered with grated cheese. Salad and fresh fruit.

Day 5: Cold tongue, baked potatoes and salad. Caramel Rice and Compote to follow.

Day 6: Sliced tongue heated up in caper sauce, with mashed potatoes and vegetable. Caramel Rice and Compote.

Day 7: Either another cold tongue meal, or, for a change, cut the tongue up into small cubes and add to savoury rice (*see* p. 87) with a few capers. Eat with any remaining salad. Finish up the fresh fruit and/or puddings.

BEEF CASSEROLE NIÇOISE

This recipe is based on one of those thick, aromatic Mediterranean dishes which smell almost better than they taste. Ideally it should be made with red wine, but thick tomato sauce with a little wine vinegar will do. Don't skip the olives unless you hate them. They give a salty, smoky flavour all their own.

2 lb. shin of beef, ¼ lb. bacon, 3 carrots, 3 onions, 3 cloves of garlic, 10–12 black olives, 1 medium tin peeled tomatoes, wine vinegar, herbs, salt, pepper

Cut the beef into thick slices. Cut bacon into small strips. Chop onions coarsely, and slice carrots thinly. Heat some oil in a casserole which can be heated over a hotplate – alternatively the fried ingredients can be transferred to a casserole before going into the oven. Put the bacon strips in, then the meat and onions. Turn the meat slices till brown all over. Add tinned tomatoes, and a dash of wine vinegar. Also the chopped garlic and carrots, bayleaf, parsley, thyme, a little rosemary, salt, pepper. Heat together till the stew simmers, then transfer to moderate oven (gas 4, 350°F., 180°C.) and cook, covered, for 2½ hours. Add the stoned olives and cook, covered, ½ hour longer. If the casserole liquid seems scanty you can add a little boiling water thickened with tomato purée. But the sauce should be thick.

Salt belly of pork is better than bacon if you can get it.

CARAMEL RICE*

This is a posher version of the standard rice pudding, with a creamier texture and a caramel glaze over the top for contrast. Some thick cream stirred in with the egg yolks makes it better still.

¼ lb. Carolina rice, 3 Tbs. sugar, ½ tsp. vanilla essence, 1 pint milk, 1½ oz. butter, 2 egg yolks, sugar for caramel

The rice should be blanched in boiling water. Throw it in when the water boils, boil 3 minutes, drain and add to the milk and vanilla. Put the rice in a moderate oven (gas 4, 350°F., 180°C.) to cook for about ½ hour, when the rice should be soft and have absorbed almost all the milk. Beat up the egg yolks and the sugar and butter and mix into the rice thoroughly. Turn the mixture into a fireproof dish or pudding basin, stand this in a baking tin half full of warm water, and cook for 20–30 minutes, or until the custard is set. Take it out and leave it to cool. When cold sprinkle a layer of sugar (caster sugar if available) over the top of the pudding. The sugar should be thick enough to hide the pudding but not inches deep. Heat the grill fiercely. Then slide the pudding under the grill till the layer of sugar caramelizes over the top. It should be like a sheet of brown glass. Cool and serve.

COMPOTE OF FIGS AND MUSCATELS

This is one recipe I have not tried, but it was given to me by a vegetarian friend who assures me that it is delicious. Dried figs and muscatel raisins are not the cheapest dried fruit, but you only need to use a few of each and this compote needs no cooking.

4–6 dried figs, a handful of muscatel raisins, sugar to taste, water

Simply put the fruit into a bowl with cold water to cover and a little sugar, and leave overnight. By the next day the flavours from the fruit will have seeped into the water and you can eat it as it is or with cream.

*   *   *

These specimen menus should give some idea of how to plan a week's eating ahead, so that you spend as little time as possible in the kitchen and, at the same time, have a reasonably varied selection of meals. There are many other recipes you can use, of course. A few alternatives are given at the end of this chapter, and you will find others elsewhere in the book. Brawn, which is very cheap and not difficult to make, is an alternative cold dish which keeps well. A rabbit would give approximately the same number of meals as a chicken, at half the cost, though the identical recipes might not all be suitable. You could casserole or bake half the rabbit, and make a pâté with the rest (see p. 169). Leftovers are good curried. Roast shoulder of lamb could be eaten hot, then cold with a well-seasoned salad, and the remains used for Suleiman's Pilaff. As a rule, fish is less suitable for this sort of cookery, because it does not keep (smoked fish excepted) and it tastes pretty nasty re-heated, though cold fish can be incorporated into a salad. Avoid steamed or baked puddings which are made to be eaten hot, otherwise you would be safe with most of the pudding recipes in this book. And, if you feel like it, you can always throw in an extra from time to time – Eggs Mayonnaise, or a Vegetable Soup.

The two points to remember, I think, are to go for foods which can be used up in a variety of ways, and avoid monotony. Most people will happily eat the same dish twice over, if it is good. After that there will be plaintive cries of 'not *again*!' Leftover dishes can be very good, but they should be well disguised, and highly flavoured.

BEETROOT SOUP (*8 helpings*)

4 raw beetroots, cleaned and peeled, 1 pint stock plus ¾ pint water and 1 chicken bouillon cube, 2 oz. butter, salt, pepper, sour cream

Grate or shred raw beetroots and cook in butter for 20 minutes. Meanwhile heat stock, water and bouillon cube to simmering point. Start adding the stock gradually to the beetroot, waiting between each addition till it has all been absorbed. Continue till the beetroot is very soft. Add any remaining stock, and simmer for ½ hour. Strain and add salt and pepper to taste. Re-heat, and stir in 3 Tbs. sour cream. You can buy sour cream in cartons, or make your own by adding a few drops of lemon juice or vinegar to ordinary cream.

GARBURE (*4–6 helpings*)

A regional French dish, well flavoured and hearty eating. The result will be something between a thick soup and a liquid stew, depending on how much water or stock you add. The basic ingredients should be haricot beans, cabbage, and some form of pork – I have used belly of pork and boiling bacon successfully. A garlic sausage ring improves the flavour too. Other vegetables which can be added, in season, are French beans, broad beans, turnips, carrots.

1 lb. belly of pork or 1 joint boiling bacon, garlic sausage, 1 cabbage, ½ lb. potatoes, ½ lb. haricot beans, garlic, salt, pepper, thyme and/or marjoram, water, or stock if you have it

Soak haricot beans overnight, or, if you are in a hurry, for a few hours in tepid water to which you have added a pinch of soda (wash beans well before cooking). Put them in cold water to cover and bring slowly to the boil. Simmer, covered, for ¾–1 hour. Now add potatoes, peeled and cut into chunks, meat left whole, herbs, 2–3 cloves garlic, salt and pepper, and any other root vegetables you may be using, peeled and cut up. If you have any stock, add it to the bean water. Simmer for 1 hour. Now add cabbage, cut into shreds, mix all the ingredients up together and cook for another ½–1 hour.

The French serve this on slices of bread. The meat is usually eaten separately, but you can please yourself.

STUFFED ONIONS/TURNIPS/CELERIAC*

All these vegetables are suitable for stuffing, and, as the method of preparation is much the same, I have lumped them under one heading for convenience. Stuffed tomatoes need slightly different treatment, so I have given a recipe for them elsewhere (*see* p. 204).

Whichever vegetable you are using, choose reasonably large ones as near the same size as possible. Scrub and peel the turnips or celeriac thinly. You can leave the onion peel on, which helps to prevent the onions bursting later.

Put the vegetables in boiling water for a few minutes – 5–6 will be enough for the onions, a couple of minutes longer for the others. This parboiling process softens them, which makes it easier to hollow the middles out, and cuts down the cooking time in the oven. Drain well. Cut a lid off the top of the vegetables and scoop out some of the inside. You can chop up the inside part and mix it with the stuffing, or mix it into the stock/tomato sauce/cider or whatever you put round them in the casserole. What you stuff them with depends on what you have to hand. Scraps of leftover meat, chicken, bacon, chopped up finely and bound with a little cooked rice, or breadcrumbs, or grated cheese. Sausagemeat, pepped up with chopped garlic, onion and parsley. Whatever you use, make sure that it is well seasoned with minced onion, garlic, chopped herbs, salt and pepper. Work a little butter into the stuffing. Fill the cavities in the vegetables, sprinkle a few breadcrumbs or a little grated cheese over the top of them, and pack them into small casserole. Pour round them some tomato sauce (*see* p. 41), stock flavoured with a few chopped vegetables, or a little cider, and bake in a moderate oven (gas 5, 375°F., 190°C.) for 45 minutes to 1 hour. From time to time, baste the vegetables with a little of the stock.

Serve with plained boiled rice and the juices from the pot.

BACON OR HAM FRITTERS (*4 helpings*)

This is a useful way of eking out a few rashers of bacon or the remains of a bacon joint, or some scraps of ham.

First make a batter with 2 oz. plain flour, ½ tsp. baking powder, salt, pepper and approximately ⅛ pint of milk. Add diced ham or bacon (fried till crisp first if you are using bacon rashers) and a little chopped parsley or spring onion tops. Stir well into the batter. Heat some oil in a pan and drop spoonfuls of the batter in, frying over moderate heat till brown on both sides.

GOULASH (*4 helpings*)

This can be made very satisfactorily with cheap cuts of meat like shin of beef, ox cheek or stewing veal. Ox cheek is the cheapest of these, it has a good flavour, not much texture, but by way of compensation is very tender when cooked long and slowly. If you use it, make sure your piece is not excessively fatty – if it is, you may need to buy rather more. Don't omit the caraway seeds, they are essential to the dish.

1 lb. shin of beef, ox cheek or stewing veal, 2 large onions, 2

cloves garlic, 1 small tin peeled tomatoes or 2 Tbs. tomato purée, 1–2 tsp. paprika, 1 tsp. caraway seeds, ¼ pint hot water, 1–1½ lb. potatoes, flour seasoned with salt and pepper, oil, butter or dripping, sour cream (optional)

Trim fat off meat and cut into cubes. Dust with seasoned flour. Peel the potatoes and keep them in cold salted water for the time being. Peel and slice the onions and chop the garlic.

Heat the butter, oil or dripping in a heavy pan, and fry the meat till brown. Add onions and garlic and cook for a few minutes longer. Now add all the other ingredients, except the potatoes, and stir well to mix. Cover the pan – if you don't have a heavy pan it might be better to transfer the dish to the oven, in a casserole, to finish cooking – and simmer over a very low flame for 2–3 hours, depending on the type of meat. Veal will take the least time, ox cheek next, and shin the longest. In any case this dish is improved by lengthy cooking. Half an hour before dishing up, boil the potatoes for 15 minutes. Cut them into quarters and add to the goulash for the last 10 minutes of cooking.

If you decide to cook the dish in the oven, set it at gas 3, 325°F., 160°C., and cook for 2½–3 hours.

Sour cream or yoghourt stirred into the goulash before serving gives an authentic Hungarian touch.

BRAWN* (*8 generous helpings*)

Brawn is a robust traditional dish which deserves to become popular again – it is exceptionally cheap, simple to do, and makes a very good cold meal with baked potatoes and salads. For the squeamish – dissecting a pig's head is not half as alarming as you might expect, once it has been thoroughly cooked.

Half a pig's head with chaps, 2 lb. ox cheek, 2 onions, 2 carrots, bayleaf, thyme, 3 hard-boiled eggs, salt, pepper

Wash the head, put it in a large saucepan, with water to cover, and bring rapidly to the boil. A lot of scum will rise (this is inevitable when boiling meat, so don't be put off), and should be skimmed off. When the scum has stopped appearing, pour off the water, rinse out the pan and add the meats, herbs and the onions and carrots sliced fairly small. Cover with water again, bring to the boil and remove any scum which the ox cheek may release. When the water has cleared, reduce heat to simmering point, and leave to cook for at least 4 hours.

Now remove meats from stock and rapidly sort the meaty chunks from fat, bone, intractable gristle and skin. Chop them into smallish cubes with a sharp knife. Boil up the stock rapidly, adding salt and pepper to taste. Strain. Cut hard-boiled eggs into halves and arrange them over the bottom of a large mixing bowl, put in the meat and pour over your stock. Stand a suitable-sized plate on top and weight it to compress the brawn. By next morning, any fat left in the meat or stock will have risen to the top, and you scrape this off before turning out the brawn, which emerges as a handsome galantine of meats, imprisoned in a transparent golden-green jelly.

SUPERIOR RHUBARB

This is an excellent way of cooking rhubarb, which could be used for other soft, juicy fruit like gooseberries. Leaving it covered in sugar overnight draws out the juices.

Cut the rhubarb into 1 inch lengths, without peeling. Put it in a fireproof dish with a cover. Add approximately 8 oz. sugar per lb. of rhubarb. Leave to stand overnight. The next day bake slowly, covered, in its own juices, in a slow oven (gas 3, 325°F., 160°C.). No water should be added. If you find the result too sweet, add less sugar the next time.

Fancy Work

The food in this chapter is intended to be slightly out of the ordinary one way or another – more extravagant, more elaborate or more exotic. For these reasons, I think of it as food for special occasions, rather than every day. You can please yourself as to what occasions you choose to call special – dinner party, anniversary, seduction scene, peace offering or simply a break in humdrum routine for the cook. Your choice of food depends on the circumstances. Chinese Pancakes would be a mistake at a rather stiff gathering of people, where your presence, all smiles and unruffled charm, is needed to keep things moving at all. A largely cold meal, which can be prepared ahead, with one hot dish needing very little last-minute attention, is in order here. Kipper Pâté, Baked Gammon and perhaps Lemon Mousse would be a good choice. Greedy friends of long standing, on the other hand, will enjoy all the brouhaha of making the above-mentioned pancakes, and probably give you a hand as well. Something light and elegant seems to be indicated for romantic evenings, Partan Pie for instance, unless instinct tells you that you are dealing with a massive appetite. Almost all men, incidentally, can be appeased by platefuls of hot and fiery food – curry, or hotter still, Chili con Carne. You must provide plenty of cold beer or lager to wash them down with.

Paupers are probably debarred by lack of cash from giving as many duty dinners (to impress the boss, visiting firemen, rich relations, chance celebrities) as other people, which is probably nicer for them, if not so good for their careers. Still, such occasions crop up from time to time and cause a disproportionate amount of anxious planning and brooding and fussing about what to eat, and what to drink, and what will they like and/or be impressed by. The rule in such cases is – never over-reach yourself. Better to provide them with an unpretentious dish you know you can cook well, and without too much agony of mind, than something untried which sounds very grand and costs so much you have to rely on the cheapest of vinegary wines to lubricate the conversation. (Rule 2 – you can happily offer cider or plonk to your friends, but never to the other category of guests. If you can't afford at least 2 bottles of a reasonable wine, it would be wiser to put the evening off.) All this may sound trite, but it is sadly true. So, if you wish to impress, don't try to be impressive. A pleasant soup to start off with, followed by a handsome-looking pie or Steak and Kidney Pudding (this homely classic has acquired considerable class, perhaps because so many people have forgotten how to make it) with appropriate vegetables (again for snob reasons, boiled sprouts score over frozen peas). Some frothy-looking confection to end up with (Apricot Fool, Orange Jelly, Strawberry Cream), quite a lot of some pleasant wine to wash it all down, and your evening of strategic socializing is off to a good start. The effect to aim for is Home-made Food as it was in the good old days, simple but well cooked, and a far cry from the tarted up pseudo-foreign cuisine they eat at expense-account lunches.

While on the subject of duty dinners, I would just like to mention another point, which seems to follow on from what I have been saying about the food, and that is – don't labour the finer points of etiquette, or you are liable to appear pretentious when you only wanted to be correct. No place cards (unless you are entertaining dozens of pompous people), no elaborate seating drill (chief guests next to host, if woman, hostess if man, and the rest shuffle into place more or less as they please), no after-dinner ceremonial like passing port, or ladies dispersing to powder their noses. These rituals are inappropriate below the butler-level, and quite ludicrous if you eat in the kitchen. Serve the coffee at the table, and if people begin to look cramped, jump up and suggest a general withdrawal to more comfortable surroundings.

CUCUMBER VICHYSSOISE (*4 servings*)

1 lb. potatoes, 1 cucumber, 1 onion, 1 Tbs. butter, 1 pint stock, salt, pepper, $\frac{1}{4}$ pint cream or top of milk

Peel and dice potatoes, peel cucumber and cut into chunks, chop onion. Heat butter in pan and add vegetables, turning them frequently till well impregnated with butter. Add the stock and cook gently till tender – about $\frac{3}{4}$ hour. Pass through a sieve, add salt and pepper. If you are going to eat it hot, add some top of milk to each serving. If you are eating it the correct way, chilled, stir in $\frac{1}{4}$ pint single cream.

A handful of watercress, or sorrel leaves can be added to the vegetables to change the flavour subtly.

GAZPACHO (*4 helpings*)

Cold, highly spiced Spanish soup. Anyone lucky enough to own an electric blender can whizz through the preparations in a few minutes. The rest must toil away with a Mouli, comforting themselves with the reflection that most Spanish cooks still pound up the ingredients in a mortar or chop them interminably till they are reduced to a pulp. You do also need a fridge because gazpacho should be served chilled.

1 lb. tomatoes, 2 cloves garlic, 1 large onion, 1 green pepper, ½ cucumber, 1 tin tomato juice, 4–6 Tbs. olive oil, 2–3 Tbs. lemon juice and/or wine vinegar, cayenne pepper

Reserve a little cucumber, onion and tomato, all peeled and chopped into cubes to serve with the soup. Then fry little cubes of bread in 1 Tbs. oil with 1 clove of crushed garlic heated in it, to add crunch.

Next, purée the remaining vegetables (tomatoes and cucumber should be peeled) and mix with the tomato juice, cayenne, vinegar or lemon juice and olive oil. It is probably best to add the last two ingredients a bit at a time, tasting frequently, to make sure the soup is neither too acid nor too oily. Add a little salt if necessary. Chill well.

Serve in bowls, in which you can if you are very grand, float a lump of ice. Guests help themselves to raw diced vegetables and croûtons.

TAPENADE

Tapenade is a sort of relish, salty and pungent, much eaten in Provence. You can spread it on thin slices of toast, eat it with cheese, on biscuits, even stuff hard-boiled eggs with it. If you like the taste of olives, you will love it. It would be a good appetizer before a meal, a change from that ersatz taramasalata made with pounded cod's roes.

¼ lb. black olives, ¼ lb. green olives, 1 Tbs. capers, 1 hard-boiled egg yolk, 10 anchovy fillets, a little fresh thyme, olive oil to moisten

A pestle and mortar, or something equivalent, are needed for the preparation.

Stone all the olives. Chop them first with a knife, then transfer to the mortar. Pound to a paste. Add the anchovy fillets, drained of their oil and wiped with a tissue. Pound till smooth. Add capers (chop them first) and egg yolk. Pound till smooth. Put in your fresh thyme (dried can be substituted) and a trickle of olive oil. The tapenade should not be liquid, just moist enough to spread easily. So add only enough oil to reach this consistency. Pack into a small jar.

STUFFED MUSSELS (4 *helpings*)

An appetizing way of serving up mussels as a light first course. You can use less garlic if you prefer.

1 quart mussels, approximately 3 Tbs. dry breadcrumbs, 3 cloves garlic, handful parsley, 1 tsp. grated lemon rind, salt, pepper, 2 oz. butter, 1 lemon

First clean the mussels thoroughly. Rinse them under running water to remove grit or weed. Pull off the beards with pliers or a strong knife. Discard any mussels that refuse to close. Rinse again. Put the mussels in a pan large enough to take them in one layer on the bottom. Place the pan over moderate heat, with the cover on, and cook for 1–2 minutes or until the mussels have opened. Half-open is enough. If the mussels are overcooked at this stage, they will be tough. Strain any liquid off into a bowl and remove one shell from each mussel.

Melt the butter in a frying pan and gently fry the bread-crumbs and finely chopped garlic, stirring till the crumbs are soft and have absorbed the butter. Remove from heat. Mix in the finely chopped parsley, a little salt, black pepper and grated lemon rind. Arrange the mussels in a flat fireproof dish and spread a little stuffing over each one. Pour over the mussel liquor, and a splash of white wine, if you have any. Put the dish into a moderate-to-hot oven (gas 5, 375°F., 190°C.) for 5–10 minutes or until they are heated through.

Serve a wedge of lemon to squeeze over each helping.

KIPPER PÂTÉ*

8 oz. packet frozen kipper fillets, 4 oz. unsalted butter, juice of ½ lemon, 2 Tbs. tomato purée or paste, black pepper

Pour boiling water over the kippers to thaw. Leave to cool. Remove the skin, mash and pound to a paste, or put through a fine sieve. Add butter, lemon juice, pepper and tomato paste, and pound till smooth. Pile up in a shallow dish and dot a few black olives around.

Serve with dry toast.

SCRAMBLED EGGS IN ASPIC* (*2–4 helpings*)

A cool, elegant-looking first course for four, or light supper dish for two. It is not at all difficult to make, though the aspic takes a little time.

4 eggs, 1 dessertspoon Parmesan or 1 Tbs. Cheddar, grated, 1 oz. butter or margarine, salt, black pepper, ½ pint aspic

Break eggs into a basin and beat lightly, adding salt, pepper and grated cheese. Melt half the butter or margarine in a pan, add eggs and remaining butter, and leave without stirring over lowest possible heat till the eggs have formed a soft crust on the bottom of the pan, without browning, however. Turn over carefully, in largest possible curds, and go on cooking very slowly till there is barely any liquid left in the pan. Turn off heat and leave the eggs to cook on in their own heat. When this mixture is set spoon on to individual saucers and leave to cool.

Now the aspic. You *can* buy ready-made aspic in a packet and mix it with hot water, adding 1 chicken bouillon cube per ½ pint water. But this really needs sherry added to it to make it interesting.

Much the best results come from making your own aspic, which is done by boiling up the remains of a cooked chicken – carcase, skin and scraps – with 1 chopped onion, 2 sliced carrots, a pinch of dried tarragon or thyme, salt and pepper. Leave this simmering till all the flesh has left the bones, then strain it and stand it in a cool place till the fat can be skimmed off. Boil up again, fast, till reduced to about ½ pint, add salt, pepper and a little soya or Worcestershire Sauce to improve the colour. Clarify the aspic by straining it through a fine cloth into a bowl, and mix in ½ packet powdered gelatine. Leave till quite cold, but not set solid, pour it over the eggs and leave to set. If the aspic is not quite cold, it will release minute fat particles from the eggs, which will cloud your clear amber jelly.

RABBIT PÂTÉ

The most frequent objections to rabbit meat are that it is dry and full of little bones. One way of getting over these difficulties is to make it into a pâté.

1 rabbit, weighing approximately 1 lb., 1 lb. belly of pork, ½ lb. fatty bacon rashers, 10 juniper berries, thyme, parsley, 3 cloves garlic, a pinch of mace, 1 tsp. grated lemon peel, 2 Tbs. cider, white wine or sherry, bayleaves

Ask the butcher to cut the rabbit into pieces. Simmer these in a little water for 25 minutes. Leave to cool. Remove all the flesh from the bones and chop, or mince, it together with the pork (from which you have removed any rind and bone), garlic, a generous handful of thyme and parsley, and the juniper berries. A mincer saves time, but diligent chopping with a sharp knife gives better results. Season the mixture with quite a lot of black pepper, pinch of mace, grated lemon rind, and a pinch of salt. Add the cider, wine or sherry. If you are not in a hurry, leave the ingredients to stand for 1–2 hours to mix the flavours well. Line the bottom and sides of a medium-sized mixing bowl, or of 2 smaller earthenware oven dishes, with the rashers of bacon, rinds removed. Pack in the ingredients. Lay 2 bayleaves on top and cover with more bacon rashers. Cover the bowl or dishes with a lid, foil or plate.

Cook standing in a pan with a little water in it, in a slowish oven (gas 3, 325°F., 160°C.) for about 2 hours or until the pâté starts coming away from the sides of the container. The cooking time will be longer in one larger container than in two smaller ones. Remove from oven. Lay a sheet of greaseproof paper on top, weight it, and leave overnight.

If you are not planning to eat it at once seal the pâté by pouring over a little melted lard.

CELERIAC SALAD (*4 helpings*)

Can be eaten on its own, as an hors d'œuvre, or with cold meat or grilled chops.

Peel the celeriac and cut it into matchstick strips with a sharp knife. Dress it rapidly, because it discolours if exposed too long to the air. The dressing used in Paris bistros, where this is a regular offering, is made with 2 Tbs. French mustard mixed with 4 Tbs. fresh cream, plus a few drops of lemon juice, salt and pepper. A mustardy mayonnaise, even a vinaigrette dressing, could be substituted.

N.B. You can parboil the celeriac for a few minutes before shredding it. Some people prefer it that way.

LEEKS VINAIGRETTE

Serve these cold, either as an hors d'œuvre, or with cold meat or chicken. Choose leeks as near as possible the same size, and allow 2 per head.

Wash the leeks carefully – steeping them upside down in cold water helps to loosen the mud and grit – and trim them to roughly the same length, keeping an inch or so of green. Plunge them into boiling salted water, and boil, covered, till tender but not mushy. The time depends on the size of the leeks – prod them with a fork to test them. Drain them very thoroughly in a colander, finishing off by patting them dry with a clean dish cloth, or tissue. Sprinkle them with a little salt, pepper and nutmeg, and douse with vinaigrette dressing. Leave to get cold.

TURKISH BITTERSWEET SALAD

Even if, like me, you tend to be sceptical about daring mixtures of fruit and vegetables in salads, you might find this one worth trying. The taste is mysterious, but nicely so, and it makes a refreshing change from the old favourites. Try it with grilled kebabs of liver or lamb.

3 large oranges, 1 large mild Spanish onion, a handful of black olives, pinch coriander seeds, paprika, olive oil, salt and pepper

Peel the oranges, ruthlessly cutting off all the pith, and slice thinly into a bowl so you save the juice. Peel and chop the onion fairly coarsely. Stone the olives. Toss in 1–2 tsp. oil till everything is well coated. Then season with salt, pepper, a good pinch of paprika and the coriander seeds. Toss again and leave in a cool place for 1–2 hours before serving.

As a change you could add some sliced rounds of chicory to the salad.

PARTAN PIE (*2 helpings*)

An excellent Scots version of devilled crab. Crabs are not cheap, but the breadcrumbs in this dish make a small crab go quite a bit further. Remember, too, that crab, like lobster, is very filling, and what looks like quite a small amount will be unexpectedly satisfying. Don't on any account omit the nutmeg which combines very well with crab.

1 crab, 2–3 Tbs. dry breadcrumbs, 1 oz. butter, 4 Tbs. wine vinegar, pinch dry mustard, nutmeg, salt, pepper

Ask the fishmonger to prepare the crab for you, or if this is not possible see directions below for doing it yourself. Put all the meat into a bowl. Mix with the breadcrumbs. If you are out of breadcrumbs, you could substitute a few crushed crackers. Heat the vinegar with the mustard, salt, pepper and a grating of nutmeg. Mix with the crab meat. Transfer to a small fireproof dish. Dot generously with butter and brown lightly under the grill.

Best eaten with a lightly dressed green salad. If you must have bulk, a few boiled potatoes.

To prepare a crab yourself, first remove the big claws. Twist off the small claws and pull off the under-shell which lies between them. Discard the small sac which lies in the top of the big shell, any green matter there, and the cluster of spongy 'dead men's fingers' lying round the big shell. Scrape out the creamy brown substance in the big shell with a small spoon – this is edible. Pick out all the white meat from the body of the crab. Crack the big claws and remove all the white meat, likewise the small claws. Mix the white and creamy brown meat together for Partan Pie.

FRESH CRAB SALAD (*4–6 helpings*)

A medium-sized crab will stretch to feed quite a few people if you mix it into a rice salad. Ask the fishmonger to clean and prepare the crab for you (or see above for how to do it yourself). When you get it home, turn all the soft meat from the shell into a bowl. Crack the claws and extract the white meat. Pick what you can from the legs.

For the salad you will need $\frac{3}{4}$–1 lb. Patna rice, boiled for

12 minutes in salted water with $\frac{1}{2}$ lemon in it. Drain the rice, wash under running hot water for a minute and dry off for a few minutes in a baking tin in a low oven. When it has cooled a little stir in vinaigrette dressing to taste, salt, black pepper and a little nutmeg. Add chopped spring onions (or shallot or chopped Spanish onion), a small packet of frozen peas cooked till tender in sugared water and drained, some thinly sliced tinned red pepper, finely chopped parsley and a few chopped chives if you have any. Add the crab meat. Stir all together thoroughly but gently with a wooden spoon, heap it up attractively in a large shallow dish, and serve with a tomato salad and, for contrast, a dish of thinly sliced cucumber drained for $\frac{1}{2}$ hour with a little salt, then dried and dressed with plain yoghourt and a squeeze of lemon juice or vinegar.

SWEET-SOUR FISH (*3–4 helpings*)

1–1$\frac{1}{2}$ lb. bream (you could substitute grey mullet or bass), salt, flour, 4 Tbs. oil

Sweet-sour Sauce: 1 small tin pineapple chunks, oil, 1 piece stem ginger in syrup, 2 Tbs. wine vinegar, 1$\frac{1}{2}$ Tbs. sugar, $\frac{1}{2}$ Tbs. tinned tomato purée, 1$\frac{1}{2}$ Tbs. soya sauce, $\frac{1}{2}$ pint water, 2 oz. finely chopped spring onions, 1 level Tbs. cornflour

First season fish with salt, inside and out, and coat with flour, making sure it sticks properly. Set oil to heat gently in frying pan large enough to take the fish (if the worst comes to the worst you can cut off the head), while you make the sauce.

In a saucepan gently fry pineapple in a very little oil. Sprinkle over finely chopped ginger. Mix vinegar, sugar, soya sauce, tomato purée, and cornflour together thoroughly, stir in water and add to pineapple. Simmer gently for 5 minutes, stirring constantly. Reduce heat to minimum.

Now fry the fish. Increase heat under the oil, lay in the whole fish and fry first one side, then the other, till brown. Turn it carefully to avoid breaking the fish. When fish is done (test by making a small incision in fattest part – flesh should be firm and white, not transparent) slide it on to a heated dish. Increase heat under sauce for a minute, adding water if it seems too thick, and add the chopped spring onions. Pour sauce over fish and serve with plain boiled rice.

CHINESE PANCAKES* (4 helpings)

This is the sort of food you would eat in Chinese homes rather than restaurants. It consists of little pancakes, dry outside, moist inside (a little like the Indian chapattis) which you daub with a thick soya sauce and roll up round a highly spiced meat ball and a couple of spring onions. Messy, but quite delicious. It is a dish which definitely requires a rehearsal or two before you spring it on your friends. It is not difficult, but it needs practice to get all the operations going successfully at once, without losing your cool. Worth trying, though, as, apart from being very good and original, it is remarkably cheap.

Pancakes: 1½ cups flour, ½ cup boiling water, salt, sesame oil

Meat Ball Filling: 1 lb. beef mince, 1 large finely chopped onion, 2 finely chopped cloves garlic, 1 Tbs. soya sauce, salt, pepper, 1 egg, 2 bunches spring onions

Sauce: 1–2 Tbs. soya sauce, 1 rounded Tbs. flour, 1½ Tbs. sugar

First prepare your sauce. Mix the ingredients together thoroughly and leave to stand in a bowl. Prepare the spring onions as for a salad and lay them in a dish. Now get the meat balls ready for frying, which should be done while you are making the pancakes, in a separate frying pan of course. They need very little attention while they are cooking so this is less difficult than it sounds.

Meat Balls
Mix all the ingredients together thoroughly, binding with the

beaten egg, and shape into small balls about the size of a walnut. Roll them in flour, and leave on a floured surface till you are ready to fry them. To fry, put some oil – roughly 1 Tbs., or enough thinly to coat the pan. Sesame oil gives the most authentically Chinese flavour but olive, or corn oil, can be substituted. Add the meat balls when the oil is hot and fry quickly on both sides. Reduce heat and cook for approximately 10 minutes each side. If your pancakes are not ready by the time they are done, put the meat balls on a wire rack covered with crinkled kitchen paper (to drain off surplus fat), and leave them in a low oven to wait (gas 2, 275°F., 140°C.).

Pancakes

Sift together the flour and salt in a deep bowl, pour on the boiling water and mix. The mixture will seem rather dry to begin with, but should end up as a dryish dough. Since flours vary in absorbency, you may need more boiling water, but use it sparingly.

Knead the dough till it stretches fairly elastically. Then put it on a floured board and pat with a rolling pin or milk bottle, till it is a long oblong roll about ¾ inch thick. Cut this across into chunks 1½ inches wide, and divide these into 1½ inch squares. Take two squares, flatten each slightly with the rolling pin, dip a finger into a saucer of oil – sesame, olive or corn oil – and smear it over one side of one square. Then clap the other square on top, like a little sandwich and roll them both out together very thin and roughly circular. Put a few drops of oil in a very flat frying pan, smoothing over with greaseproof paper to distribute the oil evenly – must be greaseproof or it will absorb the oil. When the oil is moderately hot, put in the pancake, and leave for a minute till it is light brown or a deep cream colour underneath. (If black spots appear your pan may be too hot, or the heat may be uneven.) Turn the pancake and cook the other side the same way.

The pan may need re-oiling before starting the next pancake.

When they are cooked, keep them warm by standing them on a saucer, in a colander, which is resting on the bottom of a large pan with a little water simmering in the bottom. This keeps them warm without drying them out.

Repeat the process with the pancakes, oiling the pan as needed, till you have used up all your dough.

To Serve: Put the pancakes, in their steamer, on the table, also the beef balls, soya sauce and spring onions in separate dishes. Method of eating – take one pancake, peeling the two surfaces apart to make *two*, dry outside, moist and white inside. Smear the moist side with the sauce, and wrap up your meat ball and spring onions whatever way you fancy.

N.B. If spring onions are out of season you can use ordinary onion rings.

'HOT' MEAT LOAF

A hotted up version of the standard dish, with a fiery barbecue type of sauce. Chili powder is potent stuff, so it might be as well to try half the quantity in the sauce to start with and add more if you are sure you can take it.

Meat Loaf: 1½ lb. minced chuck beef, ½ cup fresh breadcrumbs, moistened with ½ cup red wine, 2 Tbs. each finely chopped parsley, onion and celery leaves, ½ clove garlic, crushed, 1 tsp. salt, pinch paprika, and black pepper, 1 beaten egg to bind

Sauce: ½ cup tomato ketchup, ¼ cup wine vinegar, 1 Tbs. Worcestershire Sauce, 2 crushed garlic cloves, 2 tsp. chili powder, 1 tsp. salt, pinch black pepper

Make the loaf first by mixing all the ingredients together thoroughly. Shape into a loaf and lay it on a greased baking tin. Heat all the sauce ingredients together for a minute or two. Pour over the loaf. Bake for 1¼–1½ hours (gas 4, 350°F., 180°C.), basting frequently with the sauce.

Wine vinegar, or cider, can be substituted for the wine. Baked potatoes and buttered carrots are nice with this.

CHILI CON CARNE (*4–6 helpings*)

More fiery food, this time of Mexican origin. Usually a great hit with men, for some reason. Serve plenty of iced lager or, at a pinch, cider with it.

2 lb. shin of beef, ½ lb. kidney beans, 2 large onions, 1 Tbs. flour, 1 Tbs. chili powder, 4 cloves garlic, 1 pint stock or 1 pint hot water and 1 beef bouillon cube, salt

Trim fat off beef and cut into neat chunks, or slices. Fry in a little oil till brown all over. Add chopped onions and garlic, and fry over reduced heat till transparent. Add boiling stock, lower heat and simmer gently, covered, for 1 hour. Mix chili powder with 1 Tbs. flour, stir in a little liquid from the pot, mix well and add to the pot. Add a pinch of salt. Continue simmering, covered, till the meat is tender – another 1–1½ hours.

The beans, which should have been soaked overnight, should be added to the Chili con Carne about 1 hour before it is ready. You may need to add some more stock or bouillon at this stage – boiling hot again, and stir it well in to mix.

If you can get hold of a pile of chapattis, serve these as an accompaniment. Otherwise, I suggest plain boiled rice to counteract the fiery sauce. A big bowl of green salad to follow.

STEAK AND KIDNEY PUDDING (*6–8 helpings*)

An excellent dish with which to impress visiting foreigners, or suitors. It is actually rather easy to make, but doesn't look it. The quantities given make a large pudding – it might be better to try a half-size pudding first.

2 lb. stewing steak or shin of beef, 3–4 sheeps' kidneys or 1 lb.

ox kidney, seasoned flour, 8 oz. plain flour, 1 pinch salt, 4 oz. beef suet

If the kidneys smell at all rank, soak them in milk for an hour or more. Clean them well, remove all gristle, skin them and chop them small. Cut the beef into 1 inch cubes, roll them in well-seasoned flour. Now make the suet crust. Sift together the flour and salt. Cut the shredded suet into the flour, add 6–8 Tbs. water, enough to make a stiff dough. Roll this out and line a pudding basin, keeping about a third of the pastry crust to cover the top with. Put in the beef pieces and kidney haphazardly, add enough water to come within an inch of the top. Season with salt and pepper. Then put on the pastry lid. Crimp the edges together and press them down over the rim of the bowl. Place a piece of foil over the top, tied with string round the ridge at the top of the basin. Put 2 inches of water in the bottom of a large saucepan with a tight-fitting lid. If possible stand something on the bottom to rest the bowl on – an inverted saucer would do. Put the pudding in when the water boils. Cover the pan tightly and leave simmering steadily for 3–4 hours. Half an hour before the meal take the pudding out, and having removed the foil cap, put it in the oven (gas 5, 375°F., 190°C.) to brown the top. (This part is not essential, but improves the appearance.)

If the pan lid is not tight fitting you will have to check from time to time to see if the water has boiled away. It will almost certainly need replenishing with more *boiling* water.

With a trad dish like this, serve Brussels sprouts or cabbage, boiled for 5 minutes or so, well drained and braised in a little butter till tender.

FLEMISH BEER STEW (*4–6 helpings*)

The original recipe uses stewing steak, but I find shin of beef, which is much cheaper, very well suited to this dish. It has lots of flavour, makes a rich gravy, and is perfectly tender if cooked long and slowly.

2 lb. shin of beef, 2 lb. onions, $\frac{1}{2}$ pint stout, $\frac{1}{2}$ Tbs. mustard,
$\frac{1}{2}$ Tbs. brown sugar, flour, salt, pepper, 1 clove garlic, bayleaf,
parsley, thyme

Have the shin cut in thick slices. Having trimmed the fat off,
cut them into large chunks. Flour lightly and sprinkle them
with salt and black pepper.

Peel and slice the onions. Melt some fat – butter, dripping or
lard – in a frying pan and fry the onions over moderate heat till
they begin to go yellow and soft. Remove them to a plate
while you fry the meat in the same fat (add a little more if the
pan is too dry), till brown all over.

Put half the onions in a casserole. Lay the meat on top with
the garlic clove and herbs, tied into a small bundle. Cover with
remaining onions.

Mix up the stout with $\frac{1}{2}$ Tbs. mustard and $\frac{1}{2}$ Tbs. brown
sugar, a pinch of salt and black pepper, and pour over the onions
and meat. Add hot water just to cover. Put on the lid and bake
in a slow oven (gas 3, 325°F., 160°C.) for 3–4 hours.

I find buttered spaghetti or noodles, and a robust vegetable
like Brussels sprouts, are good with this stew.

CHINESE SPICED BEEF (*8 helpings*)

For this dish, you must have star anise, or aniseed, a pretty star-
shaped spice, which can be bought cheaply at Chinese food
stores and some delicatessens. It gives the meat an absolutely
unique and delicious taste and aroma. For the rest, it is a gratifyingly easy recipe to prepare, the kind you can leave quietly
cooking while you talk to your guests.

2 lb. shin of beef in one piece, 2 Tbs. oil, 1 star aniseed, 1 Tbs.
sugar, 1 Tbs. soya sauce, 4 Tbs. water, 2 cloves garlic, 2 tsp.
wine or wine vinegar, pepper, noodles

If the meat is ragged-looking, tie it up neatly with string, then brown it all over in the oil. Add the soya sauce, water, vinegar, pepper and garlic cloves (whole), and simmer slowly, covered, for 10 minutes. Now add the aniseed flower. Put the pan on an asbestos mat, cover, and cook very slowly for 1 hour. Now add the sugar, turn the meat over and simmer for another hour, covered.

To serve, boil up a lot of egg noodles in salted water. Stir a little butter and soya sauce into them, and pile up in one large dish. Take the meat out of the pan, cut the string and slice on to a warmed plate. Pour over the juices from the pan. Serve the meat and juice with the buttered noodles.

If you must serve a vegetable, it should be a Chinese-style vegetable dish – the quick-fry cabbage recipe on p. 60 could be used, minus the beef. Bean sprouts, cooked the same way, would be excellent.

BEST END OF NECK ROASTED WITH HERBS (4 helpings)

Best end of neck – the series of small cutlets at the upper end of the spine – is a nice, inexpensive cut of lamb. Ask the butcher to bone it for you.

For this recipe you need 2 lb. of meat, garlic, thyme, rosemary, bayleaf and lots of black pepper

Open out the joint and rub it with garlic, black pepper and a little salt. Chop the thyme, if fresh, and mix it with a little rosemary and a broken-up bayleaf. Sprinkle these over the surface of the meat. Then roll the joint up again, and tie it securely with three or four separate pieces of string till it forms a neat bolster. Rub salt and pepper and a little olive oil into the outside of the meat, and roast in a moderate oven (gas 4, 350°F., 180°C.) for ½ hour to the lb. Baste with the juices from the meat.

Try this with Pommes Anna and a salad of curly endive and watercress or the Turkish Salad given on p. 171.

CHICKEN COOKED IN MILK (*4 helpings*)

This is an adaptation of a recipe for cooking pork or chicken in Elizabeth David's excellent *Italian Food*. Mrs David does not suggest splitting the bird, but I find this works better, as a whole bird requires an enormous amount of milk, and, by the time the chicken is tender, the milk has not reduced to the right consistency for the sauce. A good way of making a frozen bird more interesting, without drying out the meat.

1 frozen chicken weighing approximately 2½ lb., 1 quart milk, 2 oz. butter, 2 oz. ham or bacon, 1 onion, 1 clove garlic, 6 coriander seeds, a little basil or marjoram, salt and pepper

The chicken should be thoroughly thawed out before cooking. If you are buying it ready thawed from the butcher, ask him to split it into two halves for you. Otherwise, you will have to do it yourself, using a strong pair of kitchen scissors and a sharp knife. If this seems formidably difficult cut the chicken into joints instead – remove the legs and wings, and leave the breast meat on the carcase.

Rub the chicken with salt and pepper, and a cut clove of garlic. Melt the butter in a frying pan and brown the chicken in it, together with the chopped onion, ham or bacon and finely chopped garlic. Lay the chicken pieces and the other ingredients, including all the hot butter, in a casserole or fireproof dish. In a separate pan, heat the milk to boiling point, with the coriander seeds and a pinch of basil or marjoram. Now pour it with the seeds and herbs over the chicken. Add a pinch of salt and black pepper. Bring the milk to simmering point again and keep simmering, uncovered, at a moderate pace – the milk should bubble visibly though not fiercely – for 45 minutes to 1 hour. Don't touch it during this period, and you should see a golden skin forming over the contents of the pot while the milk bubbles away underneath. At the end of this time, stir the skin into the milk, together with any crusty bits sticking to the sides of the pan. The milk will have reduced quite a bit by now, and will be getting thick. Continue simmering for another ½ hour, till the sauce has reduced to a cupful or so, watching carefully to see that it does not catch and burn.

This dish can be eaten either hot or cold. If hot, serve the chicken from the pan, as it is, with some of the thick sauce. Nice with noodles and peas. If it is to be eaten cold, lay the chicken pieces flat out on a plate and coat them carefully with the remaining sauce, before leaving them to cool.

CHICKEN MARYLAND (4 *helpings*)

What sets Chicken Maryland apart, I think, is the trimmings – corn fritters, fried bananas. Sweet potatoes, or yams, which can be bought in some large markets, in London particularly, would be an original accompaniment.

You need a young chicken cut into four joints. The butcher will do this for you.

1 Tbs. flour, seasoned with salt, pepper and paprika; egg and breadcrumbs to coat the joints in; fat for frying; a little sour cream to moisten the dish

For the trimmings: 1–2 bananas each; about 8 oz. corn kernels, fresh, tinned or frozen; 2 eggs; 1 tsp. baking-powder; ½ cup soft breadcrumbs; and seasoning for the fritters

To prepare the chicken, put the seasoned flour in a bag with the chicken pieces, and shake till well coated. Then dip in beaten egg and roll in dried breadcrumbs (*see* p. 114 for how to make your own, the packaged kind are unsuitable), till covered. Heat a generous amount of butter and oil in a pan, large enough to take all the chicken, and fry the pieces gently, turning occasionally so that they are well done all over. They will take from 30–45 minutes to cook, over moderate heat. Add a little sour cream to the juices of the pan a few minutes before serving, scraping up the debris with a wooden spoon, and leave to bubble gently.

Meanwhile, in a second frying pan, make the corn fritters. For these, you must drain the corn, if tinned, or boil it up and scrape it off the cobs, if fresh or frozen. (Two cobs would be enough.) Separate the yolks and whites of the eggs. Beat the yolks and add to the corn. Season with salt and pepper. Beat whites stiff and fold in. Now add the baking powder, and enough fresh crumbs, grated from a white loaf, to make the mixture thick and dry enough to handle. Shape into little cakes. Fry in fat till brown on both sides. Put them in a dish in the oven (gas ½, 250°F., 120°C.) to keep warm till ready. Then slice the bananas lengthwise and fry them gently in butter till soft.

If the corn fritters seem like too much of a performance, you could serve the kernels just as they are, with a little butter or sour cream stirred in, and I don't suppose anyone but a Southerner would notice the difference. But don't skip the fried bananas.

Serve the chicken on a long plate, garnished with watercress and the fried bananas. Dish the corn separately. Baked sweet potatoes, with butter, or baked plain potatoes, would be a nice easy accompaniment.

BAKED GAMMON (*4–6 helpings*)

One day, I hope, a rich relation is going to send me a whole ham to bake, Virginia style, with a glistening brown crust of molasses, mustard and vinegar, studded with cloves and surrounded by spiced peaches. It is one meat I could happily eat for weeks on end, with very little help from my friends. Meanwhile a small cut of gammon, given the same treatment and dished up with apricot halves, makes an acceptable substitute.

1 small corner of gammon (about 2½–3 lb.), 1 onion, 1 carrot,

bayleaf, molasses, mustard, vinegar, cloves, a few dried apricots

If a corner of gammon is out of your price range, try cooking one of those cuts of boiling bacon, sold in polythene packs, in the same way. Remove the polythene, tie the joint firmly with string and soak it for a few hours in cold water to remove excess salt. Then cook exactly as for gammon.

Soak gammon and dried apricots overnight in cold water. Put the meat in a pan of cold water to which you have added an onion stuck with a couple of cloves, a carrot and a bayleaf. Bring very slowly to the boil over a low flame. Keep the water only faintly simmering, and cook roughly 20 minutes to the lb. stopping a little short of the full time allowance, as the joint will be finished off in the oven. If you don't want to bake it straight away, leave the meat to cool in the cooking water – this keeps it moist and tender.

While the gammon is cooking, stew the apricot halves in a little water with 1 Tbs. vinegar and a clove or two. Drain when soft and reserve the water.

To bake the gammon, first strip off the rind with a sharp knife, leaving most of the fat. (This part does not apply to boiling bacon cuts.) Score a lattice pattern on the fat with the point of a knife and stick a clove into the middle of each little pane of fat. Mix molasses, vinegar and mustard together – the amount varies with the size of your joint, but the proportions are roughly 1 Tbs. molasses to 1 dessertspoon vinegar, 1 tsp. mustard. You can use soft brown sugar equally successfully, if you have no molasses.

Put the gammon in a baking tin and spoon the mixture over it, scooping it out of the tin and repeating the process till the fat is brown and sticky. Surround the meat with apricot halves, and bake in a moderate oven (gas 4, 350°F., 180°C.) for ½ hour or so, basting once or twice with the juices in the pan, supplemented with a little apricot water if necessary.

To serve, transfer to a large plate, with the apricots all around. Dilute the juice left in the roasting pan with a little more apricot water, heat and serve as gravy.

I think ham and gammon need only the plainest accompaniments – baked jacket potatoes, a dish of buttered peas, or a faintly bitter salad like curly endive, and lots of freshly made mustard.

RABBIT FLAMANDE (*4 helpings*)

If you can get hold of a whole rabbit, ask the butcher to draw and joint it for you. The chances are you may have to settle for frozen imported rabbit, which is usually sold cut up in joints. One saddle – the body part – should be enough for two people, or one leg each. In either case this is an excellent way of giving succulence to a meat which tends to be a little dry and insipid. (When using frozen rabbit, be sure to leave it to thaw out for a few hours at room temperature first. In emergencies, steeping in tepid water will speed thawing.)

4 rabbit joints, $\frac{1}{4}$ lb. breast of pork or fat bacon, $\frac{1}{4}$ lb. sultanas and raisins, a few prunes (optional), 24 pickling onions or 8 small onions, 1 pint cider, salt, pepper, butter, thyme, flour, sugar, vinegar

Ideally you should use a heavy iron casserole. If you haven't got one, do the preliminary frying in a frying pan and transfer the ingredients after that into a heavy saucepan on an asbestos mat. Melt 1 oz. butter in the pan, cut the pork or bacon into thin strips, and brown lightly. Transfer them to a plate and brown the rabbit all over in the same butter, adding more if it seems inadequate. Put the rabbit on the plate and brown the onions. Now return pork, rabbit and onions to the pot (or into saucepan, adding fat from pan if you are using two utensils), sprinkle 1 level Tbs. flour over them, stir to mix the flour well in and pour on the cider. Add salt, pepper, thyme (in moderation) and simmer over low heat for 1 hour. Now add washed raisins, sultanas and prunes, and simmer 1 hour more.

Just before serving, melt 3 Tbs. sugar in a small pan over low heat with 1 Tbs. vinegar. When it starts to colour, or caramelize, add it to the rabbit sauce and stir it well in.

This is such a rich, heavy dish it needs nothing but plain boiled rice with it. The cider is not essential, though it helps. Plain water will do.

PIGEON CASSEROLE (4 *helpings*)

Unless you know an obliging farmer, pigeons are not all that much cheaper than cheap chicken. On the other hand, their firm, dark meat has infinitely more flavour and interest than factory-farmed chicken. Young birds are good plainly roasted, wrapped in bacon, but if there is any doubt about their age this casserole method is a safe bet.

4 plump pigeons, $\frac{1}{4}$ lb. mushrooms, 4 rashers streaky bacon, $\frac{1}{2}$ lb. small or pickling onions, $\frac{1}{2}$–1 pint cider, stock, or water plus chicken bouillon cube, handful raisins or sultanas, thyme, bayleaf, salt, pepper, butter and flour

Chop up the bacon, rinds removed, into small squares. Pigeons and onions should first be lightly browned, separately, in that order, in a little butter. Use the same fat for all three frying operations, unless it blackens too much, in which case, wipe out the pan and add fresh butter. Put each lot aside as it is done. Stir 1 Tbs. flour into the remaining fat in the pan, pour in $\frac{1}{2}$ pint cider, stock or bouillon and bring to the boil. Simmer for a few minutes, until the sauce has thickened. If you are doing this preliminary cooking in a frying pan, you will now have to transfer everything to a casserole large enough to take the pigeons and other ingredients. Put the bacon and onion in the bottom of the casserole, then add the pigeons, sliced mushrooms, raisins or sultanas, and herbs. Pour over the stock, which should come about three-quarters of the way up the sides of the birds, and bring to the boil again. (If there is not enough stock, add a little more – hot water will do.) Add a pinch of salt and some black pepper. Cover with greaseproof paper (or foil) and the lid, and cook in a hottish oven (gas 6, 400°F., 205°C.) for 1 hour. Now remove the lid, turn the birds over and cook a further 45 minutes, uncovered. If the sauce seems very thin you can strain it off into a saucepan (leaving the pigeons and other ingredients in the casserole in the oven) and boil it fiercely for a few minutes to reduce it, before returning it to the casserole dish for serving. But this should not be necessary.

Serve with baked potatoes, or boiled rice, and peas.

PIGEON PIE (*4 helpings*)

The sort of traditional English dish which is coming back into favour, rich and hearty fare such as Mr Pickwick would have relished.

2 pigeons, ½ lb. stewing steak, 4 rashers bacon, 1 large onion, pinch dried thyme, bayleaf, ½ pint stout, 2 Tbs. wine vinegar, 1 Tbs. flour, butter or dripping, salt, pepper, ½ lb. short crust pastry, 1 beaten egg to glaze

First make the pastry (*see* p. 100) and leave to stand in a cool place for at least 1 hour.

Ask to have the pigeons split in half. Wrap each half in a rasher of bacon, rind removed. Fry chopped onion lightly in butter or dripping till transparent. Add steak, trimmed of fat and cut into neat cubes, and fry till lightly browned all over. Sprinkle on the flour, pinch of salt and black pepper, and stir for a minute or two. Pour on stout and vinegar, with a pinch of thyme and bayleaf, bring to the boil and simmer for 10–15 minutes, or until the sauce has thickened. Cover the bottom of a large pie dish or roasting pan with half the meat/onion mixture. Lay the pigeon halves on top, and cover with re- mainder of meat and juices. With a sheet of foil, cover the dish carefully, pressing the foil down round the edges, and cook in a slow oven (gas 2, 275°F., 140°C.) for 2½ hours. Take out of the oven, remove foil, and leave to cool, skimming off as much fat as possible.

Roll out the pastry, about ¼ inch thick, on a floured board, to slightly larger than the size of the pie dish. Stand an inverted egg cup in the middle of the dish to support the pastry cover. Cut a long strip of pastry from the scraps and stick this round the moistened rim of the pie dish. Moisten with milk, and lay the pastry cover on top, crimping edges with a fork. Decorate with leaf-shaped pastry cut-outs, prick a few holes with a skewer, and brush with beaten egg to glaze. Return dish to hot oven (gas 7, 425°F., 220°C.) and bake 20 minutes, or until pastry is golden, then reduce heat to gas 5, 370°F., 190°C., and bake a further 20–30 minutes.

Braised celery, a large dish of peas and redcurrant jelly would go well with this pie.

ROAST VENISON (4 *helpings*)

In spite of its aristocratic nimbus of Dukes and deer shoots, venison, surprisingly, is not an expensive meat. The best cuts cost the same as the cheapest cuts of beef. It has a strong, rich flavour, not unlike beef, but more so. A roast, marinaded loin of venison would make a luxurious dish for a dinner party. The longer you can marinade the meat the better. I find it tastes good after 24 hours, superb after 48. Use the cheapest English port, with lemon juice or wine vinegar, to counteract the sweetness. A half bottle costs the same as the cheapest wine; you only need half that, and the rest will keep.

Allow about 2 lb. loin for 4 people. Ask the butcher to joint it for you to make it easier to carve – there should be two thick little steaks per head.

Marinade: 1 large tumbler port, 1 Tbs. wine vinegar or lemon juice, 1 clove garlic, 1 onion, thyme, salt, pepper, 1 tsp. coriander seeds or juniper berries (optional)

Chop the onion and garlic, and combine with all the other ingredients. Pour over the meat, in a china mixing bowl. Cover and leave for 48 hours, if possible, turning the meat from time to time.

About 2 hours before the meal, take the meat out of the marinade and mop it dry with a pad of paper tissue. Pre-heat the oven at gas 7, 425°F., 220°C. Put the venison in a roasting pan with a little butter or oil smeared over it, and roast 10 minutes or so in the hot oven till the joint is browned. Then reduce the heat to gas 5, 370°F., 190°C., and continue roasting. Baste with a spoonful of the strained marinade from time to time. The venison will take from 1½–2 hours to cook. When it feels very tender if prodded with a fork, reduce the remaining marinade by boiling it up rapidly in a pan. Serve this, mixed with any juices from the pan, very hot as a sauce. Everything should be hot – meat, plates, sauce, so don't dawdle over the carving.

I find plain trimmings go best with very rich meat – potatoes, baked along with the venison, Brussels sprouts, and, of course, redcurrant jelly. You could mix a few boiled chestnuts with the sprouts (*see* p. 67).

POMMES ANNA★ (*4 helpings*)

1½ lb. potatoes, butter, salt, pepper, garlic

You need an earthenware oven dish with a lid for this recipe.

Rub round the inside of the dish with a cut clove of garlic, and butter it generously. Peel and slice the potatoes very thinly – about the thickness of a coin – and arrange them in layers of overlapping circles with dots of butter and plenty of salt and black pepper in between each layer. Continue till all the potatoes have been used up. Put several scraps of butter on top, more salt and pepper, and cover with a layer of buttered paper and the lid. Bake in a moderate oven (gas 5, 370°F., 190°C.) for about 45 minutes. If you are cooking a roast at the same time, you can put the Pommes Anna on the shelf below, but in that case it is wise to allow a bit longer to cook them (1–1¼ hours). Test the potatoes by jabbing with a skewer. They should be soft right through. You can remove the lid for the last 10 minutes, to brown the top, or put the dish under the grill for a minute.

The two points to remember are to be generous with butter, and to make sure the dish is adequately cooked. Half-cooked potatoes are revolting.

CELERIAC AND POTATO PURÉE

Celeriac, if you have not come across it before, is a large bulbous-looking root – it is, in fact, the root of the celery plant – with a coarse brown skin. It has the flavour of celery, but is a more manageable vegetable for dishes like this one. It also makes an excellent salad (*see* p. 170), served raw with a mustardy dressing.

For this purée you want roughly equal weights of celeriac and potato.

Scrub the celeriac, and cook, unpeeled, in water till it is quite tender. Wearing rubber gloves (the peel stains), peel and mash it, then put it through a sieve. Mix with boiled sieved potatoes. Return to the pan and beat in a good lump of butter and plenty of seasoning – salt, black pepper, a little nutmeg – over a low flame. If you have any cream, or top of milk, stir that in too.

This goes very well with the roast venison recipe (*see* p. 188), or with roast pork, grilled pork chops, or gammon.

SWEET-SOUR-LEEKS (*6 helpings*)

One of the best ways of treating leeks which brings out all their flavour. Can be served cold as a salad, or hot as an accompaniment to meat loaf, etc.

2 lb. leeks, 3 cloves garlic, 1 Tbs. sugar, 2 small lemons, cooking oil, paprika

Trim off tough green leaves and wash leeks – standing them upside down in cold water helps loosen dirt trapped between leaves. Cut into inch-long segments, dry with paper or a towel. Finely chop garlic and fry in hot oil with sugar till sugar begins to brown slightly, then add leeks, and stir and turn them till they are coated in the sugary oil. Add squeezed lemon juice, cover tightly and simmer very gently for about half an hour, till the leeks are quite tender. Plenty of juice comes out of the vegetables so no extra liquid is needed. Sprinkle with paprika before serving.

LEMON WATER ICE* (*4 helpings*)

Only for those with refrigerators. For these lucky ones, this is a pudding to pounce on. Very simple to make, elegant and refreshing, and it costs next to nothing.

1 pint water, 3 oz. lemon juice, 1 dessertspoon grated lemon rind, 1 egg white, just under ½ lb. sugar

Boil water and sugar till the sugar has melted completely. Add lemon juice and rind. Leave to cool, then strain and pour into freezing tray. Put egg white in a bowl, and place the bowl and egg whisk in fridge to get cold. When lemon ice is mushy, half frozen, beat up egg white stiffly, stir the ice with a wooden spoon, and fold in the egg white. Leave to freeze. Serve in iced glasses, very lightly rubbed (if you can manage it), with a leaf of mint.

The classic, and pleasant, accompaniment to water ices is very thin, not-too-sweet biscuits. You can buy these, or if you are feeling very energetic, make them. *See* Cinnamon Biscuits on p. 223.

CHOCOLATE MOUSSE (*4 helpings*)

Many cookbooks seem to feel the need to apologize for including a recipe for Chocolate Mousse. I don't see why, myself. It is true that it is not exactly an original offering, but it is one everyone should know – not only good to eat, but ideally simple to make.

6 oz. plain (preferably cooking) chocolate, a small lump of butter, 3 eggs, a drop of vanilla essence or rum if you have any

Melt the chocolate till soft, with a spoonful of water, in a bowl in a warm oven. Stir it, add the butter and, when amalgamated, the egg yolks and vanilla or rum. Beat the egg whites stiff, but not too dry, and fold into the chocolate mixture. Mix lightly till the mousse is uniformly brown. Pour into a shallow bowl or – if possible – into separate cups. Leave to stand overnight.

MERINGUES AND CREAM*

Home-made meringues have nothing in common with the commercial variety, which explode into brittle shards when you take an incautious bite. The home-made meringue is faintly crisp outside, tacky within and the palest honey colour. Two meringues per person, sandwiched with whipped cream and topped with a trickle of melted chocolate, are a delectable dessert, which is simple to make.

One egg white gives you four smallish meringues. But this is such a popular pudding it is best to make a few over. So for four people, allow 3–4 egg whites, 2 rounded Tbs. caster sugar to each egg white, a few drops of vanilla essence. For the filling you will need ½ pint, or medium-sized carton whipping cream, plus ½ lb. plain chocolate.

To make the meringues, beat the egg whites till they stand in peaks. Add the caster sugar a little at a time, beating constantly till the mixture is smooth and thick. Add a few drops of vanilla essence and beat briefly. Drop the mixture in spoonfuls on to a greased baking sheet, and cook in lowest possible oven till faintly tinged with colour. If you are not in a hurry it is a good idea to stand the meringues in a draught for a while to dry off *before* putting them in the oven.

To make the filling, whip up the cream till it is fluffy. You can sweeten it, but I find the plain cream contrasts well with the sweet meringue. Sandwich the meringues together with the cream. Melt the chocolate in a little water in a low oven, just before serving. Stir it till smooth, and make a little doodle over each meringue sandwich.

N.B. Meringues are the ideal way to use up leftover egg whites.

STRAWBERRY CREAM (*2–3 helpings*)

Crushed strawberries have twice as much flavour as the whole fruit, which seems to get ruddier and more insipid every year. This recipe brings out whatever taste they have. If ½ pint cream is more than you can afford, use less cream and add whipped white of egg to make up the quantity.

½ lb. ripe strawberries, ½ pint whipping cream, ½ oz. gelatine, 3 oz. sugar, juice of ½ lemon, 2 Tbs. milk

Mash the strawberries – discarding any mouldy or badly bruised ones – and push them through a hair sieve. (Plastic sieve will do, but not metal.) Stir in the sugar and lemon juice. Soak the gelatine in warm water, then melt it in the milk and strain on to the strawberry purée. Whip the cream and stir into the pulp. Transfer to a bowl or mould, and either keep in the fridge or in a cool place till needed. If you want to turn it out, smear the mould very thinly with flavourless oil first. Almond oil is the correct thing, but vegetable oil does just as well. Not olive oil, however, which has too strong a flavour.

STEAMED LEMON MOUSSE (4 *helpings*)

This is a lovely pudding, fragrant and delicate, English cooking at its most harmonious. It has a summery feel about it, but as lemons are available all the year round you could equally well serve it as a refreshing sequel to a heavy winter meal.

5 oz. butter, 6 eggs, 5 oz. sugar, 1 lemon

Separate the eggs. Put yolks, butter, sugar, juice and grated rind of the lemon in the top of a double boiler, over barely simmering water, and stir with a wooden spoon till the custard thickens. It must not boil, or the eggs will scramble with horrid results. The secret is to keep the water underneath only just simmering, and stir till the mixture reaches custard thickness, and no longer. Stir till cold (this takes less time than you would expect – a few minutes), and then fold in the stiffly beaten egg whites. Turn into a buttered or oiled (vegetable oil, not olive oil, which has too pronounced a taste) pudding basin, then cover the basin with a plate or a cap of foil. Stand it in a saucepan with an inch or so of gently boiling water in the bottom. Cover the pan itself and steam for 1 hour or so, till the mousse is firm.

Leave till cool and turn out on a dish.

ORANGE JELLY (4 *helpings*)

This makes the most delicious jelly I have ever eaten – quite different in texture from the rubberoid package type, soft and wobbly, with an incomparably fresh flavour.

9 large oranges (blood oranges are especially good), 1 lemon, 4 oz. sugar, ½ oz. gelatine

Peel thinly 1 orange and half the lemon. Boil the sugar to a syrup in a little water – about 4 Tbs. Pour on to the rind while boiling. Squeeze the juice of all the oranges, and the lemon, and strain through a hair or plastic sieve. Dissolve the gelatine in a little water, and add, together with the strained syrup, to the fruit juice. Pour into a shallow bowl or separate glasses and leave to set.

ORANGE JUMBLES

For extra panache make Orange Jumbles to eat with the jelly. 4 oz. shredded almonds, 4 oz. white sugar, 3 oz. butter, 2 oranges

Grate the rind and squeeze the juice of both oranges. Mix all the ingredients together. Grease a baking tin and drop 1 tsp. of the mixture at wide intervals, because the biscuits will spread. Bake in moderate oven (gas 4, 350°F., 180°C.). In approximately 10 minutes the jumbles will reach about the diameter of a teacup, crisp at the edges and pale in the middle. When they have cooled a little, dislodge them from the tin, roll round the handle of a wooden spoon, or rolling pin, and return to the oven for a few minutes till crisp.

GUAVA FOOL (*4 helpings*)

Tinned guavas are cheap, and puréed, they make a pleasant variation on the classic fruit fool.

1 large tin (approximately 14 oz.) guavas, ½ pint whipping cream, 2–3 Tbs. caster sugar

Drain the syrup from the guavas. Keep half a guava and put the rest through a hair sieve. Taste for sweetness. Add 2–3 Tbs. caster sugar to about the same amount of guava syrup. Mix this with the purée. Whip the cream till fluffy, and fold it into the purée. Cut the piece of whole fruit into small cubes and fold into the fool.

Pile into separate plates, or glasses, and serve.

RICE MERINGUE (*4 helpings*)

3 oz. pudding rice, 1 pint milk, 3 Tbs. sugar, 1 oz. butter, 3 egg yolks, ½ tsp. vanilla essence or 1 vanilla pod, 3 egg whites, 3–4 Tbs. caster sugar for the meringue

Cook rice with the milk and vanilla pod, or essence, in the top of a double boiler till the rice has absorbed the milk and is quite tender. Let it cool a little. Remove the vanilla pod, if you are using one. Stir in butter, sugar and well-beaten egg yolks. Turn the mixture into a buttered oven dish.

Make the meringue topping by beating up the egg whites till firm, adding the caster sugar by degrees, till the mixture is stiff and shiny. Spread it over the rice lightly but evenly, put the dish in a moderate oven (gas 4, 350°F., 180°C.) for ½ hour. If the meringue seems to be browning too much, reduce heat a little and give the pudding some extra time at the lower heat.

MONT BLANC (*4 helpings*)

A sumptuous pudding, this, and like so many of the best inventions, simplicity itself – a mound of sieved, sweetened chestnut with a cap of whipped cream. The only problem is peeling your chestnuts. This is easier if you do them while they are piping hot, but you need heatproof fingers.

1 lb. chestnuts, a little milk, vanilla sugar or sugar and vanilla essence, whipping cream

Score the chestnuts crosswise across the top – the opposite end to Brussels sprouts – and drop into boiling water. Boil for about 8 minutes. Then take out a few at a time and remove the outer shell and inner brown skin.

When you have peeled them, stew them in a little vanilla-flavoured sweetened milk till they are soft. Press them through a sieve, or small colander, so that the chestnut drops like short lengths of vermicelli on to a serving dish. Don't press this into shape, but hollow out the top and fill with cream whipped up with a little caster sugar and a drop of vanilla.

You can sprinkle the top of your Mont Blanc with grated chocolate.

PETWORTH PUDDING

You need a sweet tooth for this pudding, which could double as a tea-time offering, especially if there are children around. Keep the biscuits all roughly the same – plain or sweet.

8 oz. broken biscuits, 8 oz. plain chocolate, 1 Tbs. each currants and sultanas, 4 oz. butter, 2 Tbs. golden syrup, 2 Tbs. cocoa, 1 heaped Tbs. sugar

Melt all the ingredients, except the dried fruit, chocolate and biscuits, in a pan. Remove from heat. Add 1 heaped Tbs. currants and sultanas. Mix in the crumbled biscuits. Stir it all up well together. Pat the mixture down firmly into a flat shallow tin – flan tin perhaps. Pour 8 oz. melted plain chocolate over the top. Leave to cool. Cut into squares.

CHERRY TART (*4–6 helpings*)

One of the most beautiful-looking open fruit tarts. Make it when cherries are at their ripest and cheapest, using the dark, sweet kind. At other times you could use tinned cherries. In either case, the stones should be removed, a slightly tedious job, but it greatly improves the tart.

Short crust flan case, 1–1½ lb. dark cherries, 4 oz. sugar, 3 Tbs. redcurrant jelly

Line the flan ring with short crust pastry (*see* p. 100). Arrange the pitted cherries close together on the pastry. Sprinkle with the sugar. Bake 30–40 minutes (gas 6, 400°F., 200°C.). When the tart has cooled a little, melt the redcurrant jelly in a pan with 1 Tbs. water, and pour over the top of the cherries to glaze them attractively.

Alternatively, make a cream topping by beating together ¼ pint thick cream, 1 egg, 3 Tbs. flour and 1 Tbs. vanilla sugar or ordinary sugar, pouring this over the uncooked cherry tart and then baking for 40–45 minutes at gas 6, 400°F., 200°C., or until the top is delicately browned.

COCONUT CREAM PIE

This recipe is adapted from one of the favourites of Alice B. Toklas and Gertrude Stein. I doubt whether many people are as sweet-toothed as they appear to have been, so I have altered the proportions of the filling a little. A little fussy to make, but the result is luscious and original, especially eaten cold. The pie consists of a short crust pastry case filled with a thick vanilla cream – what the French call crème patissière – and coconut cooked till tender and transparent in sugar-and-water syrup.

Vanilla Cream: ¾ pint milk, 4 egg yolks, 3 Tbs. vanilla sugar, or plain sugar and a few drops vanilla essence, 2 level Tbs. flour

Beat sugar and egg yolks together till yellow. Add flour. When well mixed and smooth, slowly add hot milk. Put in a pan over medium heat and cook, stirring constantly, till thick. The flour prevents the mixture curdling, so it can boil – gently – without danger. Set aside to cool, adding the vanilla essence if you did not use vanilla sugar.

Coconut in Syrup: 10 oz. plain or vanilla sugar, ¼ pint water, 6 oz. grated coconut (desiccated or freshly grated)

If you are using desiccated coconut, moisten it with 1 Tbs. or so water and stir it round till absorbed.

Put sugar and water into a pan and stir over moderate heat till sugar is melted and the mixture begins to boil. Boil till slightly thickened, then stir in the coconut and continue boiling till the coconut turns into a transparent mush.

Now fill the flan case, pre-cooked at gas 7, 425°F., 220°C., for 20 minutes or until the pastry is firm, with the vanilla cream. Spoon over the syrupy coconut, distributing it as evenly as possible. Don't stir them together because if possible the coconut should rise in little peaks above the cream.

Bake in pre-heated oven (gas 4, 350°F., 180°C.) till the cream has risen a little, and is very firm, and the coconut is faintly browned on top (1 hour or slightly longer).

SOFT CHEESE WITH HERBS AND GARLIC

You can make a very reasonable substitute for that herb-and-garlic French cheese for a fraction of the price. Nice to round off a meal with, eaten on thin slices of toast.

¼ lb. cottage cheese, 1 Tbs. cream, garlic, assorted fresh herbs (thyme, tarragon, chervil, rosemary, parsley), salt, pepper

The herbs must be *fresh*. Be sparing with the rosemary, which is very pungent. Chop the herbs very finely together with 1 or 2 cloves of garlic, depending on how much you like it. Mix them into the cheese, together with the cream. Add salt and pepper to taste. Pack it all into a small pot and leave for a few hours, preferably overnight, for the flavours to develop.

Dieting on the Cheap

As most of the diets I come across seem to have been planned for overweight jet-setters, I thought it might be helpful to include some recipes for cheap, low-calorie meals. These are as nourishing, if less glamorous, than more expensive titbits – a grilled herring equals poached salmon in food value – and they are easier to stick with than drastic crash-diets.

Salads of all kinds are cheap, slimming and filling, and a dieting pauper should eat as many of them as possible, seasoned with lemon juice, plenty of fresh herbs, salt and black pepper and a few drops of oil. In winter, when the usual salad materials are expensive or poor quality, you can substitute something like coleslaw (*see* p. 202). Fresh fruit is good for filling hungry gaps between meals, especially if you nibble a small hunk of cheese at the same time.

Unless you are very pushed for time, your diet should include one hot dish a day. Too many cold meals induce revulsion after a time. Luckily, there are plenty of low-calorie, high-protein foods to choose from. Omelettes, fish, liver, kidneys, chicken are all suitable and not unreasonably priced. A small chicken should be plainly roasted, wrapped in foil part of the time to make up for the butter you won't be smothering it in, and a larger, older bird could be poached (*see* p. 140 for a recipe) and the meat eaten with slimmed-down versions of the various sauces. This way, you also get an excellent stock for soups.

I think it is important, when dieting, to keep your food as lively as possible. It would be a sensible extravagance to spend more money than usual on fresh herbs and parsley. Finely chopped, with or without garlic, these do a lot to make food more appetizing. You can add them to omelettes, stuff fish with them before baking them in foil, add them to the juices from grilled meat, and sprinkle them over the solitary baked potato allowed by less rigorous diets. (*See* p. 132 for Meal-in-a-Potato ideas.)

Puddings are difficult unless you can condition yourself to liking the taste of artificial sweeteners. A mixture of artificial sweetener and a little honey is a possibility. Some people quite like yoghourt unsweetened and I have included a recipe for making your own yoghourt, which would save a bit, with the commercial brands the price they are. On the whole, though, fresh fruit and cheese seem to be the best solutions to the pudding problem.

I think a little judicious extravagance is a good thing when one's eating is heavily restricted. Since you will be saving money on all the items you can't eat, it is sensible to spend a little extra on the things you *can*. Buy calf's liver instead of sheep or ox liver, get cod steak rather than cod fillets, the occasional piece of rump steak rather than frying steak, and so on, not forgetting the more exotic fruits in season, like peaches and pineapple. And while you will probably have had to knock off alcohol, a little wine bubbled for a couple of minutes in the grill pan where you have cooked fish or meat is rendered almost alcohol free by evaporation, but the resulting gravy will be much more appetizing.

Incidentally, where quantities are given, these are for one person, as slimming is usually something one does, grimly, on one's own.

Slimmer's salads

Here are some salad ideas you may not have tried, which you could substitute when the usual lettuce/tomato mixtures are expensive, or you are tired of them.

RAPID COLESLAW

1 carrot, ¼ white cabbage, 1 small onion, lemon juice, mustard, black pepper, salt, a few sultanas, 1 tsp. oil, herbs

Scrape and grate the carrot coarsely. Cut the cabbage into fine shreds with a sharp knife. Slice the onion into thinnest possible rings. Put all together in a bowl, adding a few sultanas (for sweetness) and any chopped herbs you happen to have. Mix the lemon juice, dry mustard and seasonings with the oil, and add, tossing the coleslaw till thoroughly coated.

This, eaten with a baked potato topped with grated cheese, or a couple of eggs baked with a little reduced meat stock, is quite a solid, warming meal. Plain grated carrot, well seasoned, is not to be despised as a quick accompaniment to grilled meat or fish.

SLIMMER'S SALADE NIÇOISE

½ cup cooked green beans (preferably stringless), 1 hard-boiled egg, 1 tomato, a few black olives, 3–4 anchovy fillets. Dressing as in previous recipe, but with 1 crushed garlic clove added

The beans should be well drained, the tomato peeled (dip in boiling hot water for 2 minutes to soften the skin), and the olives stoned for convenience. Quarter the egg and slice the tomato. Wipe the anchovy fillets to remove excess oil, and chop into small pieces. Mix the ingredients together lightly with the dressing. If you are allowed a potato, a boiled, chopped one could be added.

Good with an omelette.

RAW MUSHROOM SALAD

It may sound odd, but raw mushrooms are very good, with a delicacy of flavour often lost in cooking.

¼ lb. button mushrooms, herbs, garlic, lemon juice, salt, pepper, 1 tsp. oil

Wipe the mushrooms and cut the bottom off the stalks. Slice thinly, cover with the dressing made from other ingredients, and leave for a little time before eating, if possible. Add a little chopped fresh thyme, chives or parsley and a small amount of garlic. A very little top of milk can be added too.

Excellent with grilled meat.

BROAD BEAN AND CUCUMBER SALAD

Broad beans, when very new and small, are tender and good eaten raw as a salad. Buy ½ lb. and eat half of them cooked and half of them done like this.

Shell the beans. Slice cucumber into thin rounds or small cubes. Mix, sprinkle with fresh herbs, and season with dressing made as in the recipe above, or mixed, for a change, with 1 pounded hard-boiled egg yolk, the chopped white and a little top of milk.

A few shrimps added to this would turn it into a light meal.

STUFFED TOMATO SALAD

Cut the tops off the tomatoes and scoop out most of the inside. Sprinkle a little salt in the shell and leave to drain upside down. Meanwhile, mix together 1 chopped hard-boiled egg, a little well-drained, tinned tuna fish, some diced cucumber with plenty of fresh herbs, and dressing. Add some of the tomato pulp, and stuff the mixture into the tomato cases. A very little curry powder could be added to the dressing, also a little top of milk.

Good with a cheese omelette or scrambled eggs.

Other salad recipes given elsewhere could be adapted, such as the Turkish Bittersweet Salad (p. 171), Leeks Vinaigrette (p. 170), Celery, Beetroot and Onion (p. 74). If you really crave extra sweetness, even in salads, try adding a little fresh fruit to some of these mixtures – peeled orange segments, cubes of melon, sliced fresh peach, or pear.

Thinning soups

A well-flavoured thin soup may not sound comforting, when your stomach is crying out for a great lump of stodge, but it is a useful diet ingredient nevertheless – the warmth is soothing and seems to counteract the rather chilly acidity of endless raw vegetables and fruit. Made with a good chicken or meat stock (like the recipe given for beef tea), it is also surprisingly nourishing. French Onion Soup (*see* p. 32) eaten with the grated cheese, but not the toast or bread, is a warming meal, with a small omelette to follow.

BEEF TEA

Beef tea, a simplified form of consommé, is a nice way of getting instant nourishment when you are on a rigorous diet. You can eat it hot, or cold, when it sets to a clear jelly.

2 lb. shin of beef, 2 pints water, 1 bayleaf, pepper, pinch of salt, 1 sprig parsley, 1 small sliced onion and carrot (these are optional)

Cut the beef, from which all fat has been trimmed, into small cubes. Put them, with water and other ingredients, into an earthenware casserole and cook, covered, in a slow oven (gas 2, 300°F., 150°C.) for 3 hours or longer. (As long as your lid fits closely, this is a dish you can leave cooking in the oven at the lowest mark all day.) Strain. Leave to cool. Skim off fat. Serve cold, or re-heat.

If your diet allows it, take beef tea with slices of bread, dried till brittle in the oven. The meat can be eaten (if it still looks palatable) as a salad, mixed with hard-boiled egg, lettuce or chicory and chopped onion, and seasoned generously with lots of chopped herbs, lemon juice, salt, pepper, and as much oil as you can allow yourself.

Warning: Like all meat stocks made with vegetables this should be boiled up for 10 minutes every day to prevent it going sour. For one person, I would suggest making half the quantity given above.

VEGETABLE BROTH

1 pint stock, 2 or 3 leeks, 1 large or 2 small carrots, 1 small onion, 1 tomato or squeeze of tomato purée, a little Marmite or soya sauce, salt and pepper

Wash leeks thoroughly, peel tomato, scrape carrots. Cut all the vegetables up fairly small (the onion should be chopped not sliced) to speed up cooking. Bring stock to the boil, add all the vegetables and simmer, covered, till tender. Add a little soya sauce or Marmite, and seasoning. Eat with diet crispbread and cheese.

FRESH TOMATO SOUP

1 pint stock, ½ lb. tomatoes, 1 onion, 1 clove garlic, squeeze tomato purée, bayleaf, salt, pepper, a little cream or top of milk, chives or spring onion tops

Chop tomatoes roughly, without removing skins, and the onion and garlic quite finely. Bring stock to boiling point and add the vegetables and bayleaf. Simmer, covered, till the onion is soft. Put through a sieve and return to pan. Simmer for a minute, then taste and add salt, black pepper and a squeeze of tomato purée, if needed to intensify the flavour. Stir in a little cream or top of milk before serving, and a few chopped chives or spring onion tops.

SPINACH SOUP

Spinach soup, made with a mixture of stock and milk, is bland, pleasant and cheap.

½ lb. spinach, 1 onion, ½ pint stock, ½ pint milk, pepper, salt, nutmeg

Wash the spinach thoroughly, pulling off the largest stalks. Bring stock to the boil and add the spinach and finely chopped onion. Simmer till quite soft. Put through a sieve, and return to the pan. Now add hot milk, pepper, salt and a grating of nutmeg, and simmer for a few minutes.

* * *

I have given soup recipes elsewhere which can be adapted to diet requirements, if you cook them as above instead of in some cases frying up the vegetables in butter first. Celery Soup, Egg Drop Soup, Garlic Soup would all be suitable.

In all these recipes hot water plus bouillon cubes can be substituted for stock, though the result will not be so good. Remember to use less salt as the cubes are very salty.

BAKED EGGS*

As a change from omelettes and boiled eggs, try eggs baked like this

2 eggs, 1 slice ham, grated cheese, pepper, a little butter

You need a flat fireproof dish. Heat the oven (gas 4, 350°F., 180°C.) for a few minutes beforehand. Rub a little butter over the dish. Put the slice of ham in the bottom, having removed most of the fat, break the eggs on top. Sprinkle a little black pepper over them and 1 Tbs. grated cheese. Bake till the cheese is melted and the eggs set.

An alternative way to do eggs is to bake them in small earthenware dishes (sold as cocottes), with a little meat stock (beef tea) and a sprinkling of cheese and/or herbs.

Slimmer's fish

Fish is excellent for dieting paupers, because it is cheap, immensely rich in protein, and lends itself to non-fatty cooking methods. Grilling and baking in foil are probably the least troublesome of these, and can be used for most varieties of fish. Cod steaks, herring and mackerel are good done either way. Sprats are good grilled, with a squeeze of lemon juice. Fish like red mullet, grey mullet, fresh sardines – delicious if you can get them – are probably best grilled, with herbs and a dash of wine swilled round the pan as a sauce. As the methods for cooking are the same in all cases, barring the time factor, I shall describe the methods rather than give individual recipes.

Grilling

You need a grill pan with a detachable grid. Heat the grill beforehand. Put a little butter or oil in the grill pan with a pinch of herbs, fresh or dried, and, when the butter sizzles, add the fish, which should have been rubbed well with salt and pepper, and either opened out flat or had two slanting incisions made on either side. As soon as the fish has hit the pan, turn it over and continue grilling on this side without turning again, till it is cooked. The point of grilling like this, without the grid, is that the fish is not quite so close to the flame, so that it does not dry up. The rapid contact with the hot butter seals the side nearest the flame. Turning fish while it is cooking is hard to do without breaking it up. When the fish is done lift it up gently with a fish slice and put on a warmed plate. Add a dash of lemon juice, wine vinegar or wine (preferably white) to the juices in the grill pan, and heat over a hotplate for a couple of minutes, stirring well. Pour over fish and eat.

Herrings, mackerel and cod, i.e., fish with a strong flavour, can be rubbed with a little dry mustard before grilling.

Baking in foil

Rub the fish well with seasonings (salt, pepper, lemon juice, herbs, garlic, mustard, or whatever) and lay them on a piece of foil with a scrap of butter. Fold the foil round to prevent the juices escaping, and bake on a baking sheet in a moderate oven for 20–30 minutes, depending on the size of the fish. Open up the foil and, if the fish does not seem quite cooked, spoon a little of the juice over it and leave to cook, unwrapped, for a few minutes longer.

If your herring or mackerel has roes, you can season these with chopped herbs, minced garlic, onion, salt and pepper, and stuff the fish with the mixture before baking.

SAUTÉ OF LIVER*

Even if you have never been partial to liver, try it this way once. You may, as they say, be agreeably surprised.

¼ lb. sheep's liver, a little milk, 2 cloves garlic, 1 Tbs. chopped parsley, a little oil, salt, pepper, lemon juice

Slice the liver into thin strips and steep them in milk for an hour or two. This gets rid of any rankness of flavour. Dry carefully with tissue. Rub in salt and pepper. Heat a little vegetable oil or butter in a pan. When it is hot add the liver and stir till coloured on all sides. Now put in chopped garlic and parsley, and continue cooking over reduced heat till the liver is done, 4–5 minutes in all should be enough. The original recipe adds a few dried breadcrumbs to soak up any liquid in the pan, but this is scarcely slimming so make do with a squeeze of lemon juice.

Eat with green beans or peas, or a watercress salad with a few segments of orange mixed up in it.

Two other liver recipes which would be suitable for dieters are Liver Venetian style and Liver Kebabs (*see* pp. 57 and 129) using a modified amount of oil or butter in each case.

GRILLED MEATBALLS*

These are little meatballs, seasoned with cheese and grated onion, very savoury and tender, and since they are grilled, not too heavy on calories. You can use plain beef or a mixture of beef and pork. If possible get the butcher to mince it up for you rather than buying ready-minced meat.

For one person, ¼ lb. mince will be ample. Mix this with a little salt and pepper, 1 small grated onion and enough grated cheese to bind the mixture together. The cheese can be Parmesan, Cheddar, Caerphilly, Gruyère, etc. Shape the mixture into small balls, and grill (turn the heat down after a minute or two) not too fiercely for 10–15 minutes depending on their size, turning occasionally. It is easier to turn them if you thread them on a skewer.

Serve with any sort of salad.

STEAK TARTARE

Model girls, who have to watch their weight, are said to favour restaurants which feature Steak Tartare. It consists of raw steak scraped or grated to a soft mush, highly seasoned with chopped raw onion and capers, and bound with a raw egg yolk. (If the idea horrifies you pass on quickly.) Steak is expensive, but $\frac{1}{4}$ lb. is enough for one helping, and this is quite the most slimming way of preparing it.

$\frac{1}{4}$ lb. rump steak, 1 egg yolk, 1 Tbs. finely chopped onion and capers, salt and pepper

Either scrape the steak with a knife along the grain, which gradually breaks it down to a fibreless mush (tendons and gristle being left behind) or against a grater, which has much the same effect. *All* fat must be trimmed off previously. Season with salt and pepper. Stir in chopped onion and capers, break an egg yolk into a little dent in the centre, and eat – just as it is, preferably, or with a green salad.

DO-IT-YOURSELF YOGHOURT*

Yoghourt is healthy eating at any time and especially on a diet when you can shovel down quantities without worrying about calories. The home-made kind is so much nicer than the commercial, and so much cheaper – less than half the price – that it pays to get into a routine of making up a fresh batch every few days. I have tried all manner of yoghourt-making methods and the following is a blend of authentic Balkan know-how with Women's Institute ingenuity. I've used it time without number and never known it fail. Use a live yoghourt (Danone is the most widely available) to start the process off. A thermos is less bother than covered bowls on radiators, and handy for storage anyway – a large wide-necked thermos is easier to empty and clean and its size allows you to make enough yoghourt for several days. Decant the finished yoghourt into a bowl and store in the fridge or a cool place. It gets thicker and tastier with keeping, at its best after two or three days. Remember to reserve a spoonful to start the next batch off. It is worth buying the best grade of milk – unpasteurized gives the liveliest flavour – because the yoghourt will be that much creamier and better tasting. Dieters eat their yoghourt plain, or with a little fresh fruit sliced into it, or mixed with a little lemon juice, salt and chopped herbs as a salad dressing.

You need as much milk as your thermos will hold, plus a dessertspoonful of live commercial yoghourt. Heat the milk in a pan to boiling point and stir to prevent it boiling over for just two minutes. Leave to cool till you can dip a finger in painlessly i.e. hottish, but not scalding. Tip into thermos, scraping in the thick skin of cream on top. Add spoonful of live yoghourt, cork and cover and leave overnight – about twenty-four hours is right. Your own yoghourt culture can go on indefinitely, but remember to clean the thermos out carefully and scald it with boiling water after use.

When live yoghourt is unobtainable it is worth knowing that Long Life milk can be turned into yoghourt using *any* of the commercial brands. Plain, of course. The flavour is good but the milk costs more.

Private Enterprise

Most of the recipes in this chapter are for what might be called extras, things which are not essential, but nice to have. Jams, marmalade, sandwich spreads, biscuits and scones, soda bread, sweets. This type of cooking is fun to do when you are in the right mood. You save some money too, but the real point of home-made items like these is that they taste so much nicer than anything you could buy at a comparable price. They are a luxury paupers can afford.

Many of these recipes can be made equally well by people living in the town or country. But I have included some recipes especially for country-dwellers, because this is where private enterprise really does pay off. Without going to the lengths of buying a gun or fishing tackle, you can still supplement your eating, free, if you know where to look (ask a sympathetic local), and what to look for – a little research in the public library may help here. Quite a few good things grow wild: blackberries, of course, sloes and elderberries. Dandelion leaves for salads (the French actually grow them for the purpose), wild sorrel, highly pungent wild garlic, young nettle shoots for soup. Mushrooms take some tracking down, but they can still be found in suitable spots (hayfields where horses have been pastured are supposed to be ideal) if you get there before other people. This is one subject you must learn up though. Death caps, which look deceptively like edible mushrooms, are deadly. Safest thing is to get some knowledgeable country-man to show you the difference between the two.

Living by the sea opens up a whole new range of delicacies. Shellfish, straight from the beach and still tasting of the sea. Mussels are a lucky find, but remember that only mussels off the rocks are safe eating. Those attached to wooden groins or metal are risky, and you should check that there are no sewage outlets nearby. Other shellfish to hunt for are cockles, whelks, winkles, even limpets, but again check that they are safe eating. Standing one of the local fishermen a pint will probably supply all the information you need, and a lot more besides. A large shrimping net might be a good investment. A friend who lives on the Kent coast trails one of these along the beach, and boils up the catch – small fish, shrimps, baby crabs – into a good fish soup, bouillabaisse style, with lots of garlic and herbs, and a little cream.

Chatting up local farmers can also be helpful, and might produce an occasional hare, rabbit or pigeon, as well as odd things like buttermilk. Not for free, of course, but cheaper than shop prices.

BEETROOT AND HORSERADISH RELISH

1 lb. cooked beetroot, 1 horseradish root, 3 Tbs. vinegar, salt

Scrape and grate the horseradish root. Peel and cut the beetroot into small cubes. Mix, add 1 Tbs. each of vinegar, water and salt. Stir together, put into jam jars and seal carefully.

Good with boiled beef and any cold meat.

DANDELION SALAD*

Young tender dandelion leaves make a tasty salad either mixed up with the usual greenstuff, or on their own. If the dandelions are growing in your garden, you can make them more tender by laying a tile over the plant. With wild ones just take the youngest leaves.

Dress either with Vinaigrette (*see* p. 37), or a hot bacon dressing which is made like this.

Cut a few rashers of bacon into cubes. Put them into a pan, over moderate heat, till the fat has melted a bit and the bacon pieces are crisp. Quickly stir a spoonful of vinegar into the fat, and pour the whole lot over your salad.

N.B. This dressing also goes well with curly endive and the coarser varieties of lettuce.

GREEN BUTTER

Easily made, and nicer than most bought sandwich spreads. Useful when there are children around.

Wash and bone 2 oz. anchovies – not necessary with fillets. Boil a large handful of fresh parsley. Just cover it with water, and boil, uncovered, for about 5 minutes. Strain off the parsley and put it under the cold water tap immediately. Then strip the parsley from the stalks and chop it very fine. I find cutting it with scissors first, and finishing off with a sharp knife, is the quickest way. Now pound the anchovies to a paste, cream them together with ¼ lb. butter and the chopped parsley. This keeps for about a week in a cool place, and indefinitely in the fridge.

LEMON CURD

Until you have tried home-made lemon curd you have no idea

how good the stuff can be. Spread it on bread and butter, or use it as a sponge cake filling.

3 oz. butter, 2 large lemons, $\frac{1}{2}$ lb. sugar lumps, 3 eggs

Rub some sugar lumps over the lemons to extract the flavour from the rinds. Put all the ingredients – butter, sugar, juice from the lemons and the beaten eggs – into the top of a double saucepan and stir constantly, over just simmering water, till the mixture thickens. Pour into jars and store in a cool place.

This makes approximately $1\frac{1}{2}$ lb. curd.

Jam making

The essential article for jam making is a very large saucepan. Traditionally, these were made of copper, but an aluminium pan is just as satisfactory. It must be perfectly clean to prevent the sugar catching and burning. Where the recipe calls for warmed sugar, this means sugar which has been poured out into a large shallow baking tin and warmed in the oven for 10 minutes or so. The oven must be set at a low temperature so that the sugar does not actually melt. You can test when it is warmed by sticking your finger in. The idea of this is to ensure that the sugar melts almost instantly on contact with the hot fruit mixture.

Testing for jelling is not, I must admit, a magically simple process. The usual advice is to pour a little of the jam on to a saucer, and put it outside the window to cool off for a few minutes. If the jam is going to set, the stuff in the saucer will have formed a slight skin which wrinkles when you blow on it. Unless the recipe specifically instructs you to stop cooking after a certain time, you may need to go on testing and boiling for rather longer than indicated. It all depends on the amount of pectin (natural jelling agent) in the fruit, and this can vary with the age and quality of the fruit. When in doubt, though, it is often better to chance the jam being a little runny than boil on grimly, as the sugar does tend to burn or thicken drastically after a certain point, and jam which has to be hacked out of its containers with a stout blade is a mixed blessing. Boil, in the case of jams, means boil *hard*, unless otherwise indicated. The stuff is liable to spit and splutter, so approach it cautiously, and use a long-handled wooden spoon for stirring or testing. Having delivered all these warnings, I would just like to add that making jam satisfies some streak of the alchemist in one, in a way most cookery does not. Filling up your row of little jars (they should all be thoroughly washed, dried and warmed in a low oven) is a triumphant experience. If you are planning to keep any jams for a longish time, seal them carefully with the plastic film sold for the purpose. Otherwise, I find the screw-on lids belonging to the jars are adequate.

GOOSEBERRY JAM

Gooseberry jam is one of the easiest to make, as the fruit has a high pectin content and sets readily. If you like a slightly tart jam, it is also one of the nicest. Unripe gooseberries are best for jam as their skins are less tough.

4 lb. unripe green gooseberries, 6 lb. sugar, 1 quart water

Top and tail the berries. Put them in a large pan with 1 quart water, and bring slowly to the boil. Mash the berries with a spoon and cook on for 20 minutes. Add the sugar, previously warmed in a low oven (gas 1, 275°F., 140°C.), and allow it to dissolve. Bring to the boil. Test, after 10 minutes, by dropping a little jam on a saucer and setting it in a cool place for a minute or two. It may need 15–20 minutes to reach setting point.

These quantities will make 8–10 lb. jam. If that seems excessive, halve them.

N.B. If you can cook the berries in a copper preserving pan they will keep their green colour. Otherwise they will turn a pinkish-amber shade.

RED BLACKBERRY JELLY*

Red, unripe blackberries, sugar, water

This recipe allows you to steal a march on the other black-berry pickers.

Cover the fruit with water, and boil gently to extract the juice. Strain overnight through a muslin – the makeshift solution is to tie an old sterilized gauze nappy to the legs of an inverted kitchen chair, with a bowl standing underneath to catch the drips. Next day, measure out the juice and allow 12 oz. sugar per pint of juice. Heat the sugar in a low oven, while you bring the juice to boiling point and boil gently for 20 minutes, skimming from time to time. Now add warmed sugar to the boiling juice, and stir until dissolved and the jelly reaches boiling point again. Test to see if the jam will jell. The usual method is to drop a little on a saucer, leave it for a minute and blow on it. If it wrinkles suggesting that a skin has formed on top, it is ready. Pour into hot jars, seal and cover.

This makes a beautiful red jelly, with an excellent flavour.

SLOE JELLY*

I haven't tried this recipe, because by the time I discovered it the beautiful clusters of sloe berries, slate blue and delicately frosted, had disappeared. I am told sloe jelly tastes of plums, but rather tart.

Half-ripe sloes, a few crab apples (or ordinary apples), sugar, water

Wash half-ripe sloes. Do not dry. Put in a pan with a few quartered apples and boil gently till pulped, with a very little water. Strain through muslin overnight. To each pint of juice allow ¾ lb. sugar. Warm the sugar, heat up the juice and combine them. Boil till the jam will jell when tested. Put into small jars and store in a dark, dry place.

BRAMBLE CHEESE

Approximately equal quantities of blackberries and cooking apples, 1 lb. sugar to each pound of pulp

Wash the berries. Peel but do not core the apples. Cut them up roughly. Put in a saucepan with water almost to cover and cook slowly, covered, till reduced to a pulp. Rub through a coarse sieve, adding a little more boiling water. Weigh strained pulp and to each pound add 1 lb. granulated sugar. Stir over gentle heat till sugar is dissolved, then boil up to setting point (reached very quickly), taking care it does not burn.

Pot and seal.

This has more texture than bramble jelly, but without the seed you find in bramble jams.

SEVILLE ORANGE MARMALADE

A coarse-cut, bitter marmalade. The proportions are 1 lb. Seville oranges, 2 pints water, 2 lb. sugar

Wash the oranges and put into a covered pan with the water. Simmer slowly for approximately 1½ hours, or until a blunt wooden skewer pierces the orange skin easily. Take the oranges out of the liquid, let them cool and then cut them up into small thick strips, keeping all the pulp and juice which oozes out of them. Extract the pips, put them in the liquid, and boil steadily for 10 minutes to extract the pectin. Remove the pips and put in the cut orange pulp. Bring to the boil, and stir in the sugar, which should have been previously warmed in a baking tin in a low oven for a few minutes. Remove pan from heat and go on stirring until all the sugar is dissolved. Replace on hotplate, and boil rapidly until the marmalade reaches setting point. This may not take very long, so, to be on the safe side, start testing – dropping a little on to a saucer and blowing on it to see if it wrinkles – after ¼ hour.

These quantities yield just over 3 lb. of marmalade.

ORANGE MARMALADE

A medium-sweet marmalade.

1 lb. Seville or bitter oranges, 3 pints water, 3 lb. sugar, juice of 1 lemon

Cut or mince the oranges finely, removing the pips. Soak the peel and pulp overnight in the water, together with the pips which should be tied in a muslin bag. The next day, put the fruit, water and pips in a covered pan and simmer slowly until the peel is quite soft – approximately 1½ hours. Remove the bag of pips and stir in the warmed sugar and lemon juice. Bring to the boil, and boil rapidly, till setting point is reached – about 20 minutes.

Makes 5 lb. marmalade.

BREAKFAST MUSLI OR MUEZLI*

There seems little point buying this famous health food ready mixed when you can make your own, according to Dr Bircher-Benner's recipe, in a few minutes, and rather more cheaply.

Soak 2 or 3 Tbs. of rolled oats per person overnight in cold water. In the morning, drain them, and mix in condensed milk, raw grated apple (or other fresh fruit), a few sultanas or raisins. Add honey and lemon juice to taste.

The taste of this concoction, the *Larousse Gastronomique* adds in its dry way, is far from unpleasant.

PAIGLE FRY

Something to try for a lark during the cowslip season. You need ¼ cup cowslip heads to 1 cup pancake batter for this traditional Wiltshire dish. (*See* p. 109 for how to make the pancake batter.) Stir in the cowslip heads, cook as for pancakes and sprinkle with sugar before serving.

SUMMER PUDDING* (*4–6 helpings*)

A pudding redolent of summer. In its simplest form, it consists of nothing but blackberries, sugar and bread, but you can add apples, or substitute other soft fruit.

Simple Summer Pudding
1–2 lb. blackberries, 2–4 Tbs. sugar, stale white bread

Wash the blackberries and put into a pan with the sugar. Stew very gently till soft. Line a pudding basin with thin slices of bread, crusts removed. Fill with the fruit and juice. Cover with another layer of bread. Then lay a plate or saucer over the top, stand a weight on it to press the pudding down, and leave in a cool place or the fridge overnight.
Serve with cream.

MORE ELABORATE SUMMER PUDDING* (*4–6 helpings*)

This is made with the puréed berries (no pips) and some apples, and the bread is arranged differently, so that you get the effect of a cake rather than a pudding.

1½ lb. blackberries, 2 apples, ½ pint water, 2 Tbs. sugar, stale white bread

Peel and slice apples thinly and wash the berries. Boil the water and sugar together, till you have a thin syrup. Put the fruit into this and simmer till squashy, about 10 minutes. Pour off the juice and put the fruit through a sieve. Taste to see if it needs more sugar. Take a flat dish. Cover the bottom with very thin slices of bread, laid flat and just touching. Spoon over enough of the fruit purée to soak the bread. Continue with the layers of bread and purée till you have used up all the fruit. Finish with a layer of bread. Pour the reserved juice over the top. Press down with a weighted plate or saucer and leave overnight.

Serve with cream.

VEGETABLE PLUM PUDDING

This is a Victorian recipe, enough for sixteen people. If you want to experiment, try making a quarter the quantity to start with. The vegetable additions sound alarming but in fact they are impossible to detect in the finished dish, which has a lighter texture than most Christmas puddings.

1 lb. mashed potatoes, ½ lb. boiled and mashed carrots, 1 lb. flour, 1 lb. currants, 1 lb. raisins, 2 eggs, ¾ lb. sugar, ½ lb. shredded suet, 1 oz. nutmeg, 1 tsp. mixed spice, 1 tsp. ground ginger, a good pinch of salt

If you can add some cheap brandy or rum, the flavour will be considerably improved.

Mix all the ingredients together thoroughly in a deep bowl. To cook, either, as the Victorians did, tie up the whole lot in a well-floured wet cloth, plunge it into boiling water, and boil 4 hours. Or pack the mixture into well-greased pudding bowls, cover with greased paper and pudding cloths, securely tied down, stand in boiling water and boil 4–6 hours. When done, remove the wet cloth, tie on a dry one and leave to cool.

The first pudding must be eaten at once, the second will require 1–2 hours boiling again before use.

SODA BREAD

The traditional Irish bread, made without yeast. It is a useful standby for long Bank holidays, and other times when bread supplies might run out. A handful of currants or sultanas added to the dough make a nice tea bread, eaten with butter, hot from the oven. Ideally the bread should be made with butter milk, which can now be bought from enterprising dairies, but ordinary milk gone sour (thickened but not separated) can be substituted.

1 lb. plain flour, 1 level tsp. salt, 1 level tsp. bicarbonate of soda, 1 level tsp. sugar (optional), enough buttermilk to mix the ingredients to a dough

Sift the dry ingredients to mix. Put them in a basin. Make a well in the middle and gradually add the buttermilk, little by little, stirring in the flour at the same time, till you have a soft dough and the bowl is fairly clean. Turn on to a floured board and knead lightly. Pat dough out into a round about 1¼ inches thick. Lay it on a lightly greased baking sheet and, using a sharp knife, make a cross-shaped cut in the centre. Bake on the middle shelf of a fairly hot oven (gas 7, 425°F., 220°C.) for about 35 minutes. Remove the bread from the baking sheet and tap the bottom to make sure it is cooked through – it should sound hollow. Set it to cool or eat warm.

BUTTERMILK SCONES

Buttermilk can now be bought from good grocers and delicatessen shops and costs a little more than the same quantity of milk. You can substitute sour milk (thickened but not separated). These scones are quick and easy to make and should preferably be eaten warm from the oven. This quantity makes about 1 dozen good-sized scones.

8 oz. plain flour, 1 level tsp. baking powder, pinch of salt, 1 oz. butter or margarine, ¼ pint buttermilk, ¼ tsp. bicarbonate of soda

Sift together flour, baking powder and salt. Rub in the butter or margarine as for short crust pastry till the mixture forms fine crumbs. Dissolve the baking soda in the buttermilk and stir into the dry ingredients, till you have a soft, elastic white dough. Knead lightly till the dough is smooth and the sides of the bowl clean. Roll the dough out on a floured board, about ¾ inch thick. Stamp out into rounds about the diameter of a coffee cup. Lay these on a greased baking sheet or baking tin. Bake in a hot oven (gas 7, 425°F., 220°C.) for 10 minutes, then reduce heat to gas 6, 400°F., 200°C., and cook for another 5–10 minutes, or until the scones are lightly browned.

SUFFOLK RUSKS

9 oz. self-raising flour, ½ tsp. baking powder, pinch of salt, 3 oz. butter or margarine, 1 beaten egg, enough milk to mix

Sift the flour with the salt and baking powder. Rub in the fat to breadcrumb stage. Mix in the beaten egg and enough milk to make a light dough. Roll this out ¾ inch thick, and cut into squares. Cook in a hot oven (gas 7, 425°F., 220°C.) for 7 minutes. Remove, split them in half and return with the split sides uppermost for 10 minutes. Then dry out in a very low oven (½ gas, 225°F., 110°C.) for 30 minutes.

CINNAMON BISCUITS

The cinnamon gives these biscuits a pleasant, not-too-sweet flavour, more popular with adults than children.

3 oz. butter, 3 oz. caster sugar, 6 oz. plain flour, 1 egg, 1 tsp. powdered cinnamon

Beat butter and sugar together to a cream. Mix cinnamon into flour and gradually beat it into the creamed butter and sugar. Finally add the beaten egg and mix it all together to a stiff paste. Roll out on a floured surface and cut into rounds with a cutter or glass. Lay these on a lightly oiled baking sheet and bake in a moderate oven (gas 4, 350°F., 180°C.) for about ½ hour, or until crisp.

ORKNEY OATMEAL GINGERBREAD

Another traditional recipe – the proper name for it is Broonie – gives a nice moist plainish gingerbread, very good eaten slightly warm with butter. The oatmeal – fine oatmeal, not the coarse breakfast variety – gives it a texture not unlike fresh wholemeal bread. It is gratifyingly easy to make, even if cakes are not your strong point.

6 oz. fine oatmeal, 6 oz. plain flour, 2 oz. butter, 2 Tbs. treacle, 1 tsp. ground ginger, ¾ tsp. baking soda, 1 egg, ¼ pint buttermilk or sour milk

Sift flour, ginger and baking soda into a bowl. Add the oatmeal and mix well. Rub in the butter thoroughly. Heat the treacle till warmed and runny, and add, stirring well. Add well-beaten egg. Gradually stir in the buttermilk. Give the mixture a good stir, then turn it into a greased tin – a loaf tin is ideal – and bake in a fairly hot oven (gas 6, 400°F., 205°C.) for 1–1½ hours, or until the gingerbread is well risen and the top feels firm when you press it.

GINGERBREAD MEN

Gingerbread men, with currant eyes and buttons, have an enduring appeal for children and are fun to make. The quantities below give enough for a party – halve them for family needs.

1 lb. plain white flour, 2 oz. soft brown sugar, 2 oz. black

treacle or golden syrup, $\frac{1}{2}$ tsp. ground cinnamon and ginger,
1 tsp. bicarbonate of soda, 2 oz. butter, 1 egg yolk, currants

Heat syrup or treacle, sugar and spices together till lukewarm. Stir in butter, a piece at a time, till completely melted
then add soda. Sift flour into a deep bowl and add
mixture from saucepan, plus beaten egg yolk. Stir well till
the paste comes away from the sides of the bowl. Then turn
out on to floured board and knead lightly for a minute or
two. Roll into a ball, wrap in foil or greaseproof paper and
chill in the fridge or cool place. Roll out thinly on floured
board and cut out the shapes with a sharp knife. Decorate with
currants. Lay on greased baking sheets and bake in moderate
oven (gas 4, 350°F., 180°C.) for 20–30 minutes, or till crisp.

IRISH TEA BRACK

My twelve-year-old daughter Daisy, a connoisseur of cakes,
passed on this excellent recipe. Not strictly in the economy class
perhaps because apart from the quantity of fruit required, the
brack is so delectable it invariably disappears at one sitting. Eat
warm from the oven or cold, thinly sliced, with butter. It tastes
like a cross between soggy fruit cake and malt loaf and is
delightfully easy to make.

12 oz. raisins or sultanas, 3–4 oz. brown sugar (depending how
sweet you like cakes), 1 cup cold tea, 8 oz. brown self-raising
flour, 1 beaten egg

Brown self-raising flour (look for Farmhouse Flour) gives a
nuttier taste, but use white self-raising if you can't get it. Soak
fruit and sugar overnight in cold tea – strained, of course. Next
day mix with egg and flour, pour into greased cake or loaf tin
and bake in moderate oven (gas 5, 375°F., 190°C.) for two hours

or until a knitting-needle or knife jabbed into the cake comes out clean and not coated with brown goo.

TOFFEE SHORTBREAD

Ideal food for a children's party, a sticky cross between a biscuit and a sweet.

Shortbread: 8 oz. flour, 4 oz. butter or margarine, 2 oz. caster sugar

Rub these ingredients together to breadcrumb consistency. Press the mixture out about ½ inch thick on a baking sheet and bake for 20 minutes (gas 4, 350°F., 180°C.). Leave to cool.

Toffee: 4 oz. caster sugar, 4 oz. butter or margarine, 2 Tbs. golden syrup, 1 small tin condensed milk

Bring all these ingredients to the boil, stirring constantly, and boil for 5 minutes. Cool and spread on the shortbread.

For a finishing touch melt about 6 oz. chocolate in a double boiler with a little water and pour over the top.

When cool, cut into fingers or squares.

NUT TOFFEE

¾ lb. Demerara sugar, ½ lb. butter, 7 oz. golden syrup, grated rind and juice of ½ lemon, ¼ lb. peeled, toasted almonds or walnut halves

Boil all the ingredients together and test to see if the toffee will set by dropping a little into cold water. If ready, it will harden at once. Then pour on to an oiled tin. When just starting to set, mark off into squares with a sharp knife, loosen from the tin, and stick the nuts over the top. When set take off and break into squares. Store in an airtight tin.

CHOCOLATE FUDGE

2 lb. brown sugar, ½ pint milk, ¼ lb. butter, 3 Tbs. Van Houten's Cocoa or grated cooking chocolate, vanilla essence

Soak sugar in milk for 1 hour. Bring to the boil with the other ingredients, vanilla excepted. Boil fast for 10–15 minutes, after boiling point is reached. The mixture will rise up the pan, but do not stir more than absolutely necessary to stop it sticking and burning. Remove as soon as it begins to sink and crystallize round the sides of the pan. (This means the sugar has reached what is known as the 'thread' stage in boiling.) Leave for 2 minutes without stirring. Then put in a few drops of vanilla and beat with a wooden spoon till a smooth thick-cream consistency has been reached. Pour out on to a buttered tin, and leave to cool before cutting into squares. Store in airtight tin.

APPLE ALE

Very mildly alcoholic, refreshing and easy to make.

1 gallon cold water, 2 lb. apples (any sort), 1½ lb. sugar, 1 oz. root ginger, ½ level tsp. cloves, pinch of cinnamon

Wash apples and grate on a coarse grater. Add pulp to the water, with the cores. Stir this apple water daily for a week and then strain. Add sugar, ginger and spices and stir till the sugar is dissolved. Leave overnight. Then strain through muslin, pour off into bottles, cork lightly and leave for a week, after which the ale will be ready to drink.

LEMON BARLEY WATER

Wash 3 Tbs. pearl barley in several waters. Put a fresh quart of water with the barley into a saucepan and bring to the boil. Allow to simmer for 10 minutes. Strain the water, add juice of 2 lemons and sugar to taste.

FRIED LIMPETS

A Scottish writer of 1703 observes that 'the tender yellow part of the Limpet which is next to the Shell is reckoned good nourishment and very easie of digestion'. I have not tried them myself, but people who have tell me their taste is much like that of other small shellfish, like winkles. The two recipes which follow would, I imagine, be equally suitable for cockles, whelks and winkles, as well as limpets.

Limpets, brown breadcrumbs, salt, pepper, cayenne, fat

Collect about 2 dozen limpets per person. Wash them well to remove loose sand. Put them in a pot of water to cover and bring to the boil. Take them out, remove them from the shells, cut off and discard the tough 'feet' and wash the humps to remove any clinging sand. Roll them in the breadcrumbs, seasoned with salt, pepper and a little cayenne pepper, and fry in hot fat.

Serve with lemon slices, as a first course.

LIMPET STOVIES (*4 helpings*)

A dish traditional to the Isle of Colonsay.

2 quarts limpets, 3 lb. potatoes, water, salt, pepper, ½ lb. butter

Put the limpets in a pot with water to cover. Bring to the boil. Reserve the water. Take them out, remove them from their shells and cut off the 'feet'. Run the limpets under cold water for a minute to wash off any sand. Peel and thickly slice the potatoes. Put a layer of potatoes over the bottom of a casserole. Then a layer of limpets. Season well with salt and pepper and scatter some pieces of butter over the shellfish. Continue with layers of potato and limpets and seasoning, ending with a layer of potato. Strain the limpet water over the contents of the pot. Dot with more butter. Cover and bake in a moderate oven (gas 4, 325°F., 150°C.) for 1½–2 hours, or until the potatoes are tender.

MUTTON HAM

This is a traditional Scots recipe. In the days before refrigeration, sheep farmers cured and smoked large legs of mutton for winter use exactly as pig keepers cured and smoked their hams. Like most readers, I imagine, I have no facilities for smoking, but I have tried the curing part of the recipe on New Zealand frozen lamb and on Dorset lamb, raised and killed locally. Mutton is almost impossible to obtain unless you know a sheep farmer, and in any case, a whole mutton ham would be a lot for an average family to eat through. The better the lamb the better the ham, I would say, but even with frozen imported lamb this treatment produces a nicely flavoured joint with an attractive pink colour (the saltpetre does this) which eats very well cold for several days. Plain cold lamb I find a little tasteless. A mutton ham, or strictly speaking, lamb ham, won't taste exactly like a pork ham, but it tastes more like a pork ham than cold lamb, and I find it makes a good pauper's answer to the festive cold joint for special occasions.

1 large leg of lamb, ½ lb. salt (sea salt is best, but more expensive), 3 oz. brown sugar, ½ oz. saltpetre (most chemists stock this), 1 oz. allspice, 1 oz. black peppercorns, ¼ oz. coriander seeds.

Getting the leg boned makes your joint easier to carve, but I think the flavour is better with the bones left in. Pound all the ingredients together till the peppercorns and coriander seeds are thoroughly pulverized. (I use my coffee grinder for this, cleaning it carefully before and after of course, but you could wrap the ingredients in a cloth and bash them with a hammer, failing a pestle and mortar.) Rub the ham thoroughly and generously with the mixture, stuffing it well in round the bone. Lay the ham on a large plate, or better still, a large basin or bowl and store in a cool place (*not* the fridge) for ten days to a fortnight, basting it well every day with the dark liquid which has accumulated in the bottom of the bowl, and turning it from time to time.

To cook the ham, wipe it over with paper tissues, and put in a receptacle large enough for it to be completely submerged in water (an enamel bucket, old metal washing-up bowl, you have to use your imagination here). Cover with cold water and bring very gradually to the boil over low heat. Simmer – the water should just be moving, not bubbling furiously – for 2–2½ hours, depending on whether your leg is average-sized or large. Pour off the liquid, which will not be edible. Wipe your joint again. It will look and smell pretty nasty at this stage, but have faith. Wrap it very tightly in a clean dish cloth, safety-pinning it securely so that your joint is a neat compact shape. Put it on a tray, stand a wooden chopping board or bread board on top and a pile of weights on top of that (coffee-table books make excellent weights). Leave overnight. The next day your ham can be unwrapped, garnished as you fancy, and set out on a large platter. It will be pink inside, close textured and good eating.

N.B. Crusts of white bread dried in a slow oven and pounded make nice golden crumbs to press on to the outside of the ham, but the disadvantage is that they go mouldy before your joint is finished, very often. Likewise, chopped parsley. A sweet glaze seems less appropriate than with pork hams, but to improve the look of the ham you could try brushing honey over it and putting it in a medium oven for a few minutes, till the honey has thickened and given it a shiny coating. Baste a few times and leave to cool before serving.

Index

Index

Index

Index